Idiomatic American English

Idiomatic American English

English

A Step-by-Step Workbook for Learning
Everyday American Expressions

Barbara K. Gaines

KODANSHA INTERNATIONAL
Tokyo・New York・London

In loving memory of Grace and Dave
and
To all the negatives that made a positive.

Special acknowledgments to my daughter, Bettina, for helping me
get it all together, in more ways than one. . . .
and to my mother and father, who deserve a medal, in more ways
than one. . . .
and to my editor, Douglas LaFrenier, who, because he was on the
ball, made my work a piece of cake.

Distributed in the United States by Kodansha America, Inc., 114
Fifth Avenue, New York, N.Y. 10011, and in the United Kingdom
and continental Europe by Kodansha Europe Ltd., 95 Aldwych,
London WC2B 4JF. Published by Kodansha International Ltd.,
17-14 Otowa 1-chome, Bunkyo-ku, Tokyo 112, and Kodansha
America, Inc.

First edition, 1986
  98 99 00 15 14 13

LCC 85-82319
ISBN 0-87011-756-4
ISBN 4-7700-1256-X (in Japan)

CONTENTS

INTRODUCTION

Idiomatic expressions give English its color and vitality. They are indispensable to the daily speech of the people and to the language of newspapers and books, television and movies.

Whenever you hear a phrase whose meaning cannot be understood even if you know the definitions of the separate words involved, you have probably encountered an idiom. Mastering idioms requires a great deal of listening, studying, practice, and usage. You cannot ignore this part of the language: idiomatic expressions and more formal grammar should be given equal time. The lessons in this book are designed to teach you the kind of informal, everyday speech—including many slang words as well as idioms—that is commonly understood by all native Americans, no matter what their level of education.

There are various levels of idiomatic difficulty, and each group of lessons listed in the Table of Contents begins with the easiest lessons and ends with the more advanced ones. However, you may use them in any order you desire; each lesson is self-contained.

Each lesson begins with a dialogue, since idioms are best learned in meaningful verbal contexts. A vocabulary section then explains the idioms in clear, concise definitions. (Where the notation "neg." appears after an idiom, it means the idiom is generally used in the negative. For example, *have the heart to (neg.)* indicates the phrase is normally used in a negative statement such as "I didn't have the heart to tell her." Where alternate words are given in parentheses, either word may be used interchangeably. For example, *down the drain (tubes)* means you may say "down the drain" *or* "down the tubes."

Two sets of exercises are included in each lesson. In the first, you are asked to choose the correct idiom needed to complete a sentence. In the second, you will substitute an idiomatic expression for an italicized phrase or sentence. Be sure to choose verb endings that are appropriate to the subject and the tense, such as *I face the music, she faces the music, yesterday they faced the music.* Answers to all the exercises begin on p. 101.

Idioms fall into several categories, as indicated in the definitions:

    n.)=noun idiom. These may be simple nouns *(pad, flop),* modified nouns *(eager beaver, backseat driver),* or noun phrases *(apple of my eye, short end of the stick).*

    v.)=verb idiom. There are one-word verbs *(splurge, freeload),* two-word verbs *(rip off, count on)*, and verb phrases *(throw in the towel, face the music)*.

adj.)=adjective idiom: *cool, swamped, gung-ho, half-baked.*

adv.)=adverb idiom: *on easy street, in a nutshell, once in a blue moon.*
A few idioms are complete sentences in themselves: *The coast is clear. Mum's the word. Let bygones be bygones.*

Most idioms have precise constructions, and their whole meaning may be lost if you change them. Learn and practice them exactly as they are presented here, and listen carefully to how native Americans use them. You will soon be using them confidently yourself.

At the end of the book is a complete Glossary, listing all the idioms presented here in alphabetical order. The Glossary will help you discover the meaning of many idiomatic phrases that you hear for the first time. The lessons will help you practice them in appropriate contexts.

Idiomatic American English will help anyone who wants to have a livelier, more complete vocabulary, although students with a formal background in English will benefit the most. The goal of this book is to present a clear explanation of idiomatic expressions so that you may become more comfortable and familiar with ordinary American speech patterns and better able to express yourself in daily life.

Idiomatic American English

Lesson 1. Having a Ball

Dialogue

Tina: I feel like **having a ball.** Let's **splurge.**
Barbara: Forget it. I'm **broke.**
Tina: Don't worry. I'll **pick up the tab.** I'm **loaded** today. I'll **treat** you.
Barbara: No, we'll **go Dutch.** I don't like to **freeload.**

Vocabulary

have a ball	v.) enjoy one's self, have a good time
splurge	v.) spend a lot of money for something
broke	adj.) having no money
pick up the tab	v.) pay the bill
loaded	adj.) having lots of money
treat	v.) pay for someone else
go Dutch	v.) each pay for himself or herself
freeload	v.) get things that others pay for

Exercise I. *Complete the sentences with the correct idiom.*

a) pick up the tab   b) broke   c) loaded   d) splurge   e) treat   f) go Dutch   g) freeloads   h) have a ball

1. I don't want pizza tonight. Let's go to a fancy restaurant. Let's _____.
2. I have so much money today. I'm _____.
3. You're going to a party? _____.
4. I don't have any money. I'm _____.
5. You pay for your meal. I'll pay for mine. We'll _____.
6. This dinner was good. You don't have to pay. I'll _____.
7. She always eats dinner with us, and never invites us to eat at her house. She always

   _____.

8. Don't pay for that. I will. I'll _____.

Exercise II. *Rewrite the phrases in italics, using the proper idiomatic expression.*

1. They always *get others to pay for them.*   freeload
2. I want to *pay for* you.
3. We will *each pay our own bill.*
4. Sometimes I *spend a lot of money* on clothes.
5. After payday, *I always have a lot of money.*
6. Who *paid the check?*
7. When I go to a party, I usually *have a good time.*
8. After I pay all my bills, *I have no money.*

Lesson 2. Footing the Bill

Dialogue

Florence: I'm always **running out of** food.
Tina: Why don't you **pick up** some **odds and ends** at the store?
Florence: Because I'm **fed up with** having to **foot the bill.** I don't like to throw my money **down the drain.**
Tina: Have everyone **chip in.**
Florence: No, just **skip it.**

Vocabulary

run out of	v.) finish the supply, use up
pick up	v.) obtain, get
odds and ends	n.) miscellaneous items
fed up with	adj.) disgusted with, had enough of
foot the bill	v.) pay
down the drain (tubes)	adj. or adv.) wasted, lost
chip in	v.) contribute, give jointly
skip	v.) forget, pass over

Exercise I. *Complete the sentences with the correct idiom.*

a) runs out of   b) pick some up   c) down the drain   d) odds and ends   e) fed up with   f) footing the bill   g) chip in   h) skip

1. She doesn't like cooking every night. She's _____ it.
2. Everybody occasionally _____ bread and milk.
3. He goes to college and lives at home. He doesn't have a job yet. His father is _____.
4. I bought a pair of shoes that don't fit me. I wore them once but my feet hurt. I can't wear them anymore. That was money _____.
5. Susan wanted to go to the movies but John was too tired. She told him to _____ it.
6. I'm almost packed for vacation. I only need suntan lotion, toothpaste and other _____.
7. I don't have enough money to buy that color TV. How much do you have? If all of us _____, we can buy it.
8. I don't have any bread. I have to _____.

Exercise II. *Rewrite the phrases in italics, using the proper idiomatic expression.*

1. We *used all the* milk yesterday.
2. I must *get* a loaf of bread.
3. I'm *disgusted with* riding the subways.
4. Whenever they went for dinner, he had to *pay*.
5. If you gamble, it's money *wasted*.
6. We're buying her a gift and asking everyone to *contribute*.
7. We need some *miscellaneous items* for the party.
8. *Forget it!*

Lesson 3. Making Ends Meet

Dialogue

Barbara: You're a **clotheshorse.**
Harriet: I know. I love **dressing up.**
Barbara: Do you **shop around** a lot for bargains?
Harriet: I'm lucky. I work for a department store and I get a discount on merchandise.
Barbara: That's **great** because everything is **sky-high.**
Harriet: Yes, it's difficult **making ends meet.**
Barbara: We have to **cut corners.**
Harriet: Me too. I've **cut down on** luxuries.

Vocabulary

clotheshorse	n.) a conspicuously well-dressed person
dress up	v.) wear one's best clothes
shop around	v.) look in many stores
great	adj.) terrific, wonderful
sky-high	adj.) expensive
make ends meet	v.) balance one's budget, meet one's payments
cut corners	v.) limit one's buying
cut down on	v.) use less, reduce

Exercise I. *Complete the sentences with the correct idiom.*

a) shop around   b) great   c) clotheshorse   d) dress up   e) sky-high   f) cut down on   g) make ends meet   h) cut corners

1. She's looking for a particular dress. She can't find it so she has to _____.
2. She's too fat. She has to _____ food.
3. I have to save some money so I won't be eating in a restaurant for a while. I have to _____.
4. A lot of rich people live in that building. The rent is _____.
5. You're getting a raise. That's _____.
6. I made $300 but I spent $400. I can't _____.
7. She dresses very well. She's a _____.
8. Your clothes look terrible. We're going out to dinner. Why don't you take a bath and _____.

Exercise II. *Rewrite the phrases in italics, using the proper idiomatic expression.*

1. I'm *looking* for a television.
2. Rents in New York City are *very expensive.*
3. That's a *terrific* idea.
4. I *got all my debts paid* this month.
5. I'm spending all my money. I must *limit my buying.*
6. He must *reduce* the number of cigarettes he smokes.
7. She is *always very well dressed.*
8. Whenever company comes to their house, the children must *wear their best clothes.*

Lesson 4.   Raking It In

Dialogue

Florence: He was in the casino and started to **make a bundle.** He was really **raking it in.**
George: I bet he thought he **had it made.**
Florence: Then he started **losing his shirt.**
George: With his temper, he probably **hit the ceiling.**
Florence: Sure. The casino **took him to the cleaners.**
George: Was he a **good sport?**
Florence: Oh no. He was a **sore loser.**

Vocabulary

make a bundle	v.) make a lot of money
rake it in	v.) make a lot of money
have it made	v.) be sure of success, have everything
lose one's shirt	v.) lose all one's money
hit the ceiling	v.) get angry
take someone to the cleaners	v.) win all of someone's money, cheat someone
good sport	n.) person who loses well
sore loser	n.) person who gets angry when he loses

Exercise I. *Complete the sentences with the correct idiom.*

a) rake it in   b) made a bundle   c) hit the ceiling   d) lost his shirt   e) sore loser   f) good sport
g) has it made   h) took him to the cleaners

1. He has a terrific wife, lots of money, a good job, a lot of friends. He _____.
2. He went to Las Vegas and came back without any money. He _____.
3. When he lost the tennis match, he wouldn't shake his opponent's hand. He's a _____.
4. When his son got a poor grade in school, the father _____.
5. When it's very hot in the summer, ice cream stores _____.
6. He bought that stock at $1 a share and sold it ten years later at $100 a share. He
_____.

7. Even though he lost, he was happy for the winner because he deserved the prize. He's a
_____.

8. He invested money in a business deal that was bad. They _____.

Exercise II. *Rewrite the phrases in italics, using the proper idiomatic expression.*
1. He *is very fortunate. He has everything.*
2. Don't play with him. He *gets angry if you win.*
3. He's *making a lot of money now.*
4. The owner of the ski lodge *makes a lot of money* when it snows.
5. If you bother him, he'll *get angry.*
6. Bob *cheated him out of his money.*
7. He *bet all his money and didn't win.*
8. I don't mind playing cards with him. *If he loses, he doesn't get angry.*

Lesson 5. Caught Short

Dialogue

Karen: At the end of the week, I'm always **caught short.**
Joanne: That's because **money burns a hole in your pocket.** I don't **feel sorry for** you.
Karen: How can I **tighten my belt?**
Joanne: You're going to have to **do without** in order to **get along.**
Karen: I know. I'll try **brown bagging** it. Within a short time I'll be **in the chips** again.

Vocabulary

caught short	adj.) having an insufficient supply (especially of money) when needed
burn a hole in one's pocket	v.) to be spent quickly
feel sorry for	v.) pity
tighten one's belt	v.) economize, spend and use less
do without	v.) live without something
get along	v.) manage
brown bag	v.) bring one's lunch from home
in the chips	adj.) having plenty of money

Exercise I. *Complete the sentences with the correct idiom.*

a) money burns a hole in her pocket   b) tighten his belt   c) feel sorry for   d) caught short   e) do without   f) in the chips   g) brown bag   h) to get along

1. Sometimes I don't have enough cake when company comes over. I'm _____.
2. She studied so hard for that exam but she failed it. I _____ her.
3. As soon as she gets some money she has to spend it. _____.
4. Arthur lost his job. He's going to have to _____.
5. I can't find a new car in my price range. I think I'll have to _____ one.
6. He has a large family to support. It's not easy _____ on his salary.
7. He went to work on the holiday but all the restaurants were closed. He had to _____ it.
8. His family is very prosperous. They're _____.

Exercise II. *Rewrite the phrases in italics, using the proper idiomatic expression.*

1. He's trying to save money so he's *taking his lunch to work.*
2. She's on a diet. She *can't have* ice cream.
3. They have a lot of problems. I *pity* them.
4. The bill came to $25 but I only had $20 with me. I *didn't have enough.*
5. They have a beautiful home. They're *wealthy.*
6. My car is being repaired. I have to *manage* without it for a while.
7. I'm not making enough money. I'm going to have to *economize.*
8. *As soon as he gets some money, he spends it.*

Lesson 6.   An Arm and a Leg

Dialogue

Diane: That car is in **A-1** condition, but it would cost **an arm and a leg.**
Tina: I didn't know you were **in the market for** another car.
Diane: I'm thinking about it, but **for the time being,** I'll use this **jalopy.** It'll do **in a pinch.**
Tina: I'm sure a new one will **set you back** 10 **grand. That ain't hay!**

Vocabulary

A-1	adj.) excellent
set one back	v.) cost
an arm and a leg	n.) a large amount of money
in the market for	adj.) wanting or ready to buy
for the time being	adv.) at the present time
jalopy	n.) old car usually in poor condition
in a pinch	adv.) okay when nothing else is available
grand	n.) $1,000
That ain't hay!	That's a lot of money.

Exercise I. *Complete the sentences with the correct idiom.*

a) in the market for   b) for the time being   c) in a pinch   d) that ain't hay   e) grand   f) set me back
g) an arm and a leg   h) jalopy   i) A-1

1. I exercise every day and I'm in _____ shape.
2. I finally bought a fur coat but it _____ $3,000.
3. A gold watch costs _____.
4. Newlyweds are usually _____ a new house.
5. It's not time for dinner and I'm hungry. _____ I'll just have a candy bar.
6. When a teenager buys a car, he usually can only afford a _____.
7. If you don't have a needle to sew something together, a safety pin will do _____.
8. It will cost you more than one _____ to fly to Australia. You have to admit _____.

Exercise II. *Rewrite the phrases in italics, using the proper idiomatic expression.*

1. Five *thousand dollars? That's a lot of money.*
2. All I seem to find are *old cars in bad condition.*
3. Sending a child through college today can cost parents *a lot of money.*
4. *I want to buy* a very good leather jacket.
5. There was no food in the house except for a dozen eggs. I don't like eggs that much but I eat them *when there's nothing else.*
6. I just had a big lunch so *at the present time* I'm not hungry.
7. I bought a used typewriter. It's in *excellent* condition.
8. I'm sure that new car *cost him* a lot of money.

Lesson 7.   A Nest Egg

Dialogue

Stan: He's always **squawking about** money.

Jim: If he had a **nest egg,** he wouldn't have to worry.

Stan: It's difficult to **salt away** money today.

Jim: That's true. And he tries to **keep up with the Joneses.**

Stan: Not really. He tries to save, but the family expenses are **on his shoulders.** That's why he's **on pins and needles.**

Jim: Why doesn't he play the lottery?

Stan: Because he can **bank on** the fact that he's not going to **make a killing** that way.

Vocabulary

squawk about	v.) complain about
nest egg	n.) extra money saved
salt away	v.) save, keep hidden until needed
keep up with the Joneses	v.) try to equal your neighbors' lifestyle
on one's shoulders	adj. or adv.) one's responsibility
on pins and needles	adj.) nervous, excited
bank on	v.) count on, be sure of
make a killing	v.) gain a large amount of money at one time

Exercise I. *Complete the sentences with the correct idiom.*

a) salts away   b) keep up with the Joneses   c) made a killing   d) squawks about   e) nest egg   f) bank on   g) on his shoulders   h) on pins and needles

1. Anybody who goes into the army _____ the food.
2. When you retire at 65 years old, it's good to have a _____.
3. He wants a new car, so every week he _____ some money.
4. He's getting married tomorrow. He's _____.
5. Many years ago, he bought stock at $10 a share. It's now worth $1,000 a share. He sold it and _____.
6. The cost of real estate will go much higher. You can _____ that.
7. If his neighbor gets a new car, he does too. He thinks he has to _____.
8. Any president has the problems of his country _____.

Exercise II. *Rewrite the phrases in italics, using the proper idiomatic expression.*

1. He *made a large amount of money* in real estate.
2. School children always *complain about* having a lot of homework.
3. He's waiting to hear if he got the job. He's *very nervous.*
4. *Anything her neighbor has, she wants.*
5. It's always nice to have *extra money available.*
6. If you make a lot of money, you're going to have to pay a lot of taxes. You can *count on* that.
7. *He's responsible for all the work in his office.*
8. He's going to retire in a couple of years. He *saved* money so that he would have it when he needed it.

Lesson 8.   Falling Behind

Dialogue

Cindy: I'm **breaking my neck** at two jobs so I don't **fall behind** in my bills.

Gilda: Maybe you better **face up to** the fact that you can't enjoy life **to the hilt.**

Cindy: I'll **go over** my budget again. Don't **fly off the handle** if my check **bounces.**

Gilda: I'm sure it will **clear** but if you want, I'll give you some money to **tide you over.**

Vocabulary

break one's neck	v.) try very hard
fall behind	v.) not be able to keep up, fail to maintain a schedule or rate of speed
face up to	v.) accept something unpleasant or difficult
to the hilt	adv.) completely, to the limit
go over	v.) examine
fly off the handle	v.) get angry
bounce	v.) not be acceptable because of insufficient funds in the bank (said of checks)
clear	v.) go through, meet the requirements
tide someone over	v.) help someone through a shortage

Exercise I. *Complete the sentences with the correct idiom.*

a) breaking his neck   b) bounced   c) face up to   d) fall behind   e) to the hilt   f) tide you over
g) cleared   h) go over   i) flew off the handle

1. I didn't study my lesson tonight. I hope I don't _____.
2. I didn't have enough money in the bank and my check _____.
3. I know your landlord is raising your rent and you're unhappy. Nevertheless, you must _____ your situation.
4. I got so angry. I _____.
5. I know you need some extra money. Here's $25 to _____.
6. Please _____ your English papers as we're having a test.
7. I hope that big check _____. I forgot to make a deposit today.
8. He borrowed all this money on his house. He's mortgaged _____.
9. He studies very hard every night. He's _____ to get into the university.

Exercise II. *Rewrite the phrases in italics, using the proper idiomatic expression.*

1. I hope that check *goes through*.
2. It's too bad he *got angry*.
3. I'm spending too much money on groceries. I better *examine* my shopping list.
4. Sometimes you need money to *help you in bad times*.
5. He's losing his hair but he doesn't want to *accept* this unpleasant fact.
6. Bob didn't have enough money in his checking account. His check *came back*.
7. He has used his credit cards *to the limit*.
8. She has company coming for dinner and she's *working very hard*.
9. I can't work as fast as my co-workers. *I can't keep up with their pace.*

Lesson 9. When the Chips Are Down

Dialogue

Tom: I can't believe I'm **down and out.** I'm living **hand to mouth** and **pinching pennies.**

Pat: You can always **turn to** me **when the chips are down.**

Tom: I don't want any **handouts.** I don't **mooch** off anyone.

Pat: Just **sit tight.** You'll **get out from under.**

Vocabulary

down and out	adj.) having no money, no success
hand to mouth	adv. or adj.) barely able to cover daily expenses
pinch pennies	v.) be thrifty, careful how you spend money
turn to	v.) go to for help
when the chips are down	adv.) at the worst time, when one faces the biggest obstacles
handout	n.) charity
mooch	v.) borrow, beg, get without paying
sit tight	v.) wait patiently
get out from under	v.) end a worrisome situation

Exercise I. *Complete the sentences with the correct idiom.*

a) get out from under   b) turn to   c) mooch   d) sit tight   e) down and out   f) hand to mouth

g) pinching pennies   h) when the chips are down   i) handout

1. It's terrible to see those old men on a corner asking people for a _____.
2. He lost his job last week and now his family is living _____.
3. Someday he wants his own business so now he's saving and _____.
4. She needs money. Her parents are the only ones she can _____.
5. You only know your true friends _____.
6. He used to be very successful, but he gambled it away. Now he's _____.
7. He never buys his own cigarettes but he'll _____ from everyone else.
8. If you work hard enough in that company someday you'll be an executive. Just _____.
9. I know you have a lot of bills but with your new raise, you should be able to _____.

Exercise II. *Rewrite the phrases in italics, using the proper idiomatic expression.*

1. I know you're anxious but you'll just have to *wait patiently.*
2. He's always trying to *get something without paying for it.*
3. He doesn't like to get anything from *charity.*
4. He asked me for money *when he was in a crisis.*
5. He's *a failure now.*
6. They have no money saved. *They can just pay their bills from day to day.*
7. *He's very careful how he spends money.*
8. He lost his job. Who can he *go to* for help?
9. He's going to be able to *pay his bills* because he won the lottery.

Lesson 10.   Keeping One's Head Above Water

Dialogue

Tony: I'm **racking my brains** to find a way to **keep my head above water.**

Edward: I didn't know you were **hard up.**

Tony: I **put up a good front** but I haven't **seen daylight** for a long time.

Edward: I'll give you some **moola** to **bail you out.**

Tony: That's just **a drop in the bucket.** I need too much to get **back on my feet.**

Vocabulary

rack one's brains	v.) try hard to think or remember
keep one's head above water	v.) be able to exist on one's income, pay bills
hard up	adj.) in desperate need of something
put up a good front	v.) pretend to be happy, fool people about one's status
see daylight	v.) achieve or expect a favorable result
moola	n.) money
bail one out	v.) help
a drop in the bucket	n.) a small amount
back on one's feet	adj.) financially independent or physically healthy again

Exercise I. *Complete the sentences with the correct idiom.*

a) bail him out   b) get back on his feet   c) keep his head above water   d) hard up   e) racking his brains   f) a drop in the bucket   g) see daylight   h) put up a good front   i) moola

1. He works in advertising and is constantly _____ to think of creative ideas.
2. I'd like to borrow some money because I'm _____ right now.
3. He finds it difficult supporting a family and trying to _____.
4. I have so much work. I don't know when I'll _____.
5. How much _____ would that car cost?
6. Whenever he gets in trouble, his parents always _____.
7. I saved up $100 toward a new car but that's just _____.
8. She was very upset over a poor grade but didn't want anyone to know. She smiled and _____.
9. He lost everything in a fire but he is working two jobs now trying to _____.

Exercise II. *Rewrite the phrases in italics, using the proper idiomatic expression.*

1. After her husband died, she found it difficult *supporting herself,* but now she is *independent again.*
2. He's always getting in trouble and his parents have to *help him.*
3. He is too busy studying and writing papers, but soon *it will all be over.*
4. He can't find a job. He is really *desperate.*
5. I'm *trying very hard* to remember his name.
6. I need $1,000. $10 is just *a small amount.*
7. Anyone who hires his own jet has a lot of *money.*
8. *She's a good actress.* You never know if she is having personal problems.

Lesson 11.　One for the Books

Dialogue
Bill:　　He's a **nitwit**. What **half-baked** idea does he have now?

Walter:　He's sure he can become a millionaire by buying 100 lottery tickets. He thinks it'll be **a piece of cake.**

Bill:　　That's **one for the books.** It's no **cinch** making money.

Walter:　He **talks through his hat.** You have to **take** everything he says **with a grain of salt.**

Bill:　　Just watch. He'll **have egg on his face.**

Vocabulary
nitwit	n.) idiot
half-baked	adj.) foolish, silly
a piece of cake	n.) easy
one for the books	n.) very unusual, remarkable
a cinch	n.) easy
talk through one's hat	v.) make exaggerated or inaccurate statements
take with a grain of salt	v.) listen with skepticism
have egg on one's face	v.) be embarrassed

Exercise I. *Complete the sentences with the correct idiom.*

a) a piece of cake　b) nitwit　c) cinch　d) half-baked　e) egg on his face　f) take it with a grain of salt　g) talking through her hat　　h) one for the books

1. He says he got all A's in college. I don't believe it. You have to _____.
2. I can finish this work in no time. It's _____.
3. She hates to be around children and she's an elementary school teacher. That's _____.
4. He said he was sick and stayed home from work. When a co-worker saw him at a baseball game, he had _____.
5. He was going to Europe, but forgot to get a passport. What a _____.
6. At the sales meeting, he proposed a new project, but it was a terrible, _____ suggestion.
7. She's always talking about how much money she's investing and making in the stock market but I think she's _____.
8. Working that machine is not difficult. When I show you, you'll realize it's a _____.

Exercise II. *Rewrite the phrases in italics, using the proper idiomatic expression.*

1. I didn't realize they heard what I said. *I was very embarrassed.*
2. You *can't believe any of his statements.*
3. That's *so easy.*
4. That's *not hard.*
5. I can't believe he passed that difficult course without studying. That's *remarkable.*
6. He's *an idiot.*
7. He says he's so successful with women. I doubt it. He's *exaggerating.*
8. That's a *foolish* idea.

Lesson 12.   An Eager Beaver

Dialogue
Mike: That **guy** is an **eager beaver**. He never **goofs off**.
Eric: He really wants to **get ahead**.
Mike: You can **count on** him.
Eric: If extra work **crops up**, he will **pitch in**.
Mike: He's not a **clockwatcher**.

Vocabulary
guy	n.) man
eager beaver	n.) ambitious, zealous, hard worker
goof off	v.) not want to work, be lazy
get ahead	v.) become successful
count on	v.) depend, rely on; trust
crop up	v.) happen quickly without warning
pitch in	v.) help
clockwatcher	n.) person in a hurry to leave work

Exercise I. *Complete the sentences with the correct idiom.*
a) goofs off   b) pitch in   c) cropped up   d) get ahead   e) count on   f) eager beaver   g) guy   h) clock-watcher

1. He studies hard and works late. He really wants to _____.
2. He studies hard and works late. He is an _____.
3. He drinks coffee all day long and talks to his girlfriend on the phone. He _____.
4. I need more help around the house. Everyone must _____.
5. I have to stay at work late tonight. Some new work just _____.
6. He can't wait until 5:00 P.M. every day. He's a _____.
7. If you're in trouble, you can usually _____ your parents.
8. You don't have the correct change for the phone? Ask that _____.

Exercise II. *Rewrite the phrases in italics, using the proper idiomatic expression.*
1. That man is *someone who wants to work hard and do a good job.*
2. You can *depend on* a good friend in time of trouble.
3. He wants to *become successful.*
4. He *never wants to work.*
5. John will always *help* when you are busy.
6. Unexpected work will sometimes *happen without warning.*
7. He's *always in a hurry to leave at 5:00 P.M.*
8. He's a nice *man.*

Lesson 13. Bringing Home the Bacon

Dialogue
Judy: Today I'm **under the weather**.
Ann: **Play hooky**. I won't **spill the beans**.
Judy: I can't. I'm **swamped** with work. My job is **no picnic**.
Ann: Well, **hang in there**. **In the long run**, you'll be **sitting pretty**.
Judy: I hope so. I have to **bring home the bacon**.

Vocabulary
under the weather	adj.) not feeling well
play hooky	v.) stay away from school or work without permission
spill the beans	v.) tell a secret, inform
swamped	adj.) overwhelmed
no picnic	adj.) not pleasant
hang in there	v.) be patient, wait
in the long run	adv.) in the end, as a result
sitting pretty	adj.) in a favorable situation
bring home the bacon	v.) earn the family's income

Exercise I. *Complete the sentences with the correct idiom.*
a) brings home the bacon   b) no picnic   c) under the weather   d) swamped   e) hang in there
f) spilled the beans   g) played hooky   h) in the long run   i) sitting pretty

1. It's the busy season and I'm _____ with work.
2. Raising children today is _____.
3. His wife works and he stays home and takes care of the children. She _____.
4. Get a college education because _____ you'll make more money.
5. I can't go to work today. I'm getting a cold and feeling _____.
6. She didn't know about the surprise party until somebody _____.
7. The children didn't go to school. They _____.
8. She married a very nice, rich, handsome man. Now she's _____.
9. I know you want to go and have fun with your friends, but _____ and finish your homework.

Exercise II. *Rewrite the phrases in italics, using the proper idiomatic expression.*
1. *I don't feel very well.*
2. *I have too much work.*
3. Her husband died. Now she has to *support the family*.
4. They worked very hard and now *they have a good life*.
5. His wife was planning a surprise birthday party and by mistake his best friend *told him*.
6. He didn't feel like going to school today, so he *stayed out* and went to a movie instead.
7. I know you'll get the job you want. Just *be patient*.
8. He works outside. It's *not pleasant* in the winter time when it's cold and icy.
9. You should get a leather wallet instead of a plastic one because *in the end*, leather is superior.

Lesson 14.   On a Shoestring

Dialogue
Mike: **Out of the blue,** he opened up a business **on a shoestring.**
Eric: That's **a feather in his cap.**
Mike: I hope he doesn't **take a beating.**
Eric: I don't think so. He **struck while the iron was hot.**
Mike: He'll probably **wind up** being very **well-heeled.**
Eric: I hope so. He's been **through the mill.**

Vocabulary
out of the blue	adv.) unexpectedly, by surprise, from nowhere
on a shoestring	adv.) with very little money
feather in one's cap	n.) proud achievement
take a beating	v.) lose money
strike while the iron is hot	v.) take advantage of an opportunity
wind up	v.) end, finish
well-heeled	adj.) rich
through the mill	adj.) experienced in difficulties of life

Exercise I. *Complete the sentences with the correct idiom.*
a) strike while the iron is hot   b) took a beating   c) a feather in your cap   d) out of the blue
e) well-heeled   f) wind up   g) through the mill   h) on a shoestring

1. You need a lot of capital to open up a business today. No longer can you do it _____.
2. She's had a difficult life. She's been _____.
3. He was always such a happy child. Now that he's a man, how did he _____?
4. Her father can buy anything. He's _____.
5. Ask him for money on payday. _____.
6. When you finally get that promotion, it will be _____.
7. He bought that stock at $100 a share and sold it at $50 a share. He _____.
8. I didn't know he was seriously dating a girl. _____, he told me he was getting married. I was surprised.

Exercise II. *Rewrite the phrases in italics, using the proper idiomatic expression.*
1. He started business *with very little money.*
2. She's *had a very difficult life.*
3. What time did the party *finally end?*
4. He *lost a lot of money* in Las Vegas.
5. She visited me *unexpectedly.*
6. That was *a very proud achievement* for my firm.
7. I think you should *take advantage of this opportunity.*
8. He's *very rich.*

Lesson 15.   A Pep Talk

Dialogue
George: He gave them a **pep talk** and told them they better **shape up** or they'll get a **pink slip**.
Fred: I knew he'd **get around to** it. If you were **in his shoes**, you wouldn't have **let it ride**.
George: **Off the record**, I'm glad he **clamped down** on them. How are things now?
Fred: Everyone's **gung ho**.

Vocabulary
pep talk	n.) a talk to arouse enthusiasm
shape up	v.) begin to act and look right
pink slip	n.) notice of dismissal
get around to	v.) finally find time to do something
in someone's shoes	adv.) in another person's place or position
let it ride	v.) continue without changing a situation
off the record	adv.) privately, unofficially, not for public announcement
clamp down	v.) become stricter
gung ho	adj.) enthusiastic, eager

Exercise I. *Complete the sentences with the correct idiom.*
a) get around to   b) in his shoes   c) shape up   d) pep talk   e) pink slip   f) let it ride   g) gung ho
h) clamp down   i) off the record

1. He was not a good employee and they decided to let him go. He got his _____.
2. They are very enthusiastic about the project. It is a good sign when everyone is _____.
3. He takes two-hour lunch breaks and leaves work early. I think he is going to have to

   _____.
4. You cannot pass judgment on someone else unless you put yourself _____.
5. The students aren't doing their homework. I think the teacher will have to _____.
6. I haven't written that letter yet. I'll _____ it.
7. There's no enthusiasm in this group. I think we're going to need a _____.
8. Don't say anything to him right now. I don't want to hurt his feelings. _____.
9. Don't tell anyone. Keep this _____.

Exercise II. *Rewrite the phrases in italics, using the proper idiomatic expression.*
1. I'm *really enthusiastic*.
2. I think parents should *be stricter*.
3. *I don't think we should change anything for now.*
4. The boss wants the work done now, not when you *find time for* it.
5. Her appearance is preventing her from getting a promotion. It's time she *began to look right*.
6. Do I have to give this group *a speech to get some enthusiasm*?
7. What I'm going to tell you now is *private*.
8. I wouldn't like to be *in his position*.
9. He was not doing his work well and they decided to *dismiss him*.

Lesson 16. In Seventh Heaven

Dialogue

Lee: I'm **in seventh heaven.**

Kelly: I noticed your **head was in the clouds.**

Lee: I think I **made a hit with** the boss. My idea **knocked him dead.** Now he knows I **mean business.**

Kelly: I have to **hand it to you.** You **stuck to your guns** and everything **panned out.**

Lee: I'm glad I **kept my fingers crossed.**

Vocabulary

in seventh heaven	adv.) very happy
have one's head in the clouds	v.) be daydreaming, lost in thought
make a hit	v.) be successful
knock one dead	v.) greatly impress, surprise
mean business	v.) be serious
hand it to someone	v.) acknowledge, give credit to
stick to one's guns	v.) to defend an action or opinion despite an unfavorable reaction
pan out	v.) happen favorably
keep one's fingers crossed	v.) wish for good luck

Exercise I. *Complete the sentences with the correct idiom.*

a) head is in the clouds   b) stick to your guns   c) in seventh heaven   d) means business   e) kept his fingers crossed   f) have to hand it to him   g) knocked the guys dead   h) made a hit   i) pan out

1. He didn't think he'd pass that examination, so he _____.
2. When he discovered he received an excellent grade on the examination, he was _____.
3. She had company for dinner and served lobster. It _____.
4. She's in love and her _____.
5. She looked beautiful at the party and _____.
6. He made a million dollars on a small investment. You _____.
7. You didn't get the promotion? I'm sorry things didn't _____.
8. If you believe in something, it's necessary to _____.
9. I see he's ambitious. You can tell by his attitude he _____.

Exercise II. *Rewrite the phrases in italics, using the proper idiomatic expression.*

1. *I hope I have good luck.*
2. I will *not change my ideas* on that subject.
3. *I'm very serious.*
4. That movie *was successful* with the audience.
5. I'm *very happy.*
6. I'm sorry. *I'm daydreaming.*
7. That is a sexy dress. It *greatly impressed him.*
8. She raised 10 children all by herself. You have to *give her credit.*
9. I'm sorry *there wasn't a more favorable outcome.*

Lesson 17.   A Brainstorm

Dialogue
Pete: He **thought up** a great idea for a new product.
Luke: Maybe with this **brainstorm,** he'll **take the plunge** and start his own business.
Pete: I think he wants to **try his idea out** for a while. He doesn't want to **jump the gun.**
Luke: He should **kick it around** a while but it won't work unless he can **take over.**
Pete: Well, so far none of his plans have managed to **get off the ground.**

Vocabulary
think up	v.) invent, create
brainstorm	n.) very smart idea
take the plunge	v.) do something decisive
try something out	v.) test
jump the gun	v.) start before you should
kick something around	v.) discuss, think about
take over (take charge)	v.) take control, command
get off the ground	v.) make progress, a good start

Exercise I. *Complete the sentences with the correct idiom.*
a) kick it around   b) brainstorm   c) jump the gun   d) get off the ground   e) thought it up   f) try it out   g) take the plunge   h) takes over

1. When the President dies, the Vice-President _____.
2. That's very smart. Who _____?
3. Before you buy that car, _____.
4. Michael isn't making too much money now. He's waiting for his new business to _____.
5. Whose great idea was it to have a surprise party? What a _____.
6. You'll need more facts before you go into business. Don't _____.
7. I always wanted to own a jewelry store. I think this year I'll _____.
8. The boss didn't want to make the decision by himself. He wanted to _____ with his employees first.

Exercise II. *Rewrite the phrases in italics, using the proper idiomatic expression.*
1. Edison *invented* hundreds of things.
2. I've avoided taking that chemistry class, but I guess I have to *do it, finally.*
3. It's not a good idea to *to start anything before you're properly prepared.*
4. Sometimes it's necessary to *test products* before you buy them.
5. That's really a *great idea.*
6. He hopes his new business *has a successful beginning.*
7. When the boss dies, his son will *be in control.*
8. Let's *all discuss it* before we decide.

Lesson 18. The Cream of the Crop

Dialogue

Steve: He's a **brain.**
Richy: I can't **stand** him. He **rubs me the wrong way.**
Steve: Why? He's **on the ball** and **has his feet on the ground.**
Richy: What we need is someone who **keeps his nose to the grindstone.**
Steve: I read his application and he is **the cream of the crop.**
Richy: Do you think he'll get the job?
Steve: Yeah, it's **in the bag.**

Vocabulary

brain	n.) intelligent person
stand (neg.)	v.) tolerate, like
rub one the wrong way	v.) annoy, bother, make angry
on the ball	adj.) paying attention and doing things well
have one's feet on the ground	v.) be practical, sensible, stable
keep one's nose to the grindstone	v.) always work hard, keep busy
cream of the crop	n.) the best of a group, top choice
in the bag	adj.) certain, sure, definite

Exercise I. *Complete the sentences with the correct idiom.*

a) in the bag   b) cream of the crop   c) stand   d) rubs me the wrong way   e) brain   f) feet on the ground   g) on the ball   h) keep his nose to the grindstone

1. It's certain that he's going to win the election. It's _____.
2. If we're busy, he'll never leave work early. He'll _____.
3. If you graduate from a top university with good marks, future employers will think you are the _____.
4. He has tremendous knowledge. He is a _____.
5. She is going to be a good wife and mother because she has both _____.
6. She knows everything about her job. She's _____.
7. Don't give me liver for dinner. I can't _____ it.
8. What an annoying person. She _____.

Exercise II. *Rewrite the phrases in italics, using the proper idiomatic expression.*
1. He'll ask her to marry him. It's *definite*.
2. She's *an intelligent person*.
3. That university only takes the *most qualified*.
4. She *works every minute of the day*.
5. He *is very sensible*.
6. That woman *annoys me*.
7. I *don't like* loud music.
8. Ask her what happened at the meeting. *She always pays attention.*

Lesson 19. Pulling Strings

Dialogue

Bernie: There's a job opening in my company. It would suit you **to a T.**

Harold: Could you **pull some strings** to get me hired?

Bernie: I can't. **My hands are tied.**

Harold: Don't you know anyone who could **throw his weight around?**

Bernie: What about your brother? He's a **big shot.** Maybe he could **put in his two cents.**

Harold: Asking him is **wasting my breath.** I think I'll have to **make my own way.**

Vocabulary

to a T	adv.) perfectly, exactly
pull strings	v.) secretly use influence and power
One's hands are tied.	One is unable to help.
throw one's weight around	v.) use one's influence in a showy manner
big shot	n.) important person
put in one's two cents	v.) give one's opinion
waste one's breath	v.) speak or argue with no result
make one's own way	v.) rely on one's own abilities

Exercise I. *Complete the sentences with the correct idiom.*

a) throw his weight around   b) make his own way   c) my hands are tied   d) to a T   e) pull some strings   f) put in his two cents   g) wasting your breath   h) big shot

1. He always has something to say. No one asked him to _____.
2. He had no help from anyone. He had to _____.
3. He has a lot of money and influence. He's a _____.
4. You want Japanese food? Terrific. That suits me _____.
5. I don't want to pay that parking ticket. My uncle is a judge. Maybe he could _____.
6. I would like to lend you money but we just bought a house and car. _____.
7. He is always showing how important he is. He makes promises to everyone. He likes to

_____.

8. When you try to advise teenagers what to do, you are _____.

Exercise II. *Rewrite the phrases in italics, using the proper idiomatic expression.*

1. He always worked hard. *Nobody ever helped him.*
2. He always has to *give his opinion.*
3. That suit fits you *perfectly.*
4. He'll *use his influence* to help his family.
5. He likes to *use his power.*
6. He's a *very important person.*
7. I wanted him to help me with the meeting but *he's too busy and can't.*
8. He drives his car too fast, but when you tell him he'll get a ticket, *he doesn't listen.*

Lesson 20. In the Swing of Things

Dialogue
Mike: I'm going to get a promotion.
Pam: You're **pulling my leg!**
Mike: No. I deserve it. I **worked my fingers to the bone.**
Pam: I'm glad they **gave you a break.**
Mike: Finally things are **looking up** for me. I'm **taking on** more responsibility.
Pam: Now you have to get **in the swing of things** and **learn the ropes.**
Mike: It'll be **a breeze.** I'm really **cut out** for this work.

Vocabulary
pull someone's leg	v.) trick, playfully tease, fool
work one's fingers to the bone	v.) work very hard
give someone a break	v.) give someone an opportunity or chance
look up	v.) improve, get better
take on	v.) begin to handle, commit oneself to, accept
get in the swing of things	v.) adapt or adjust to a new environment
learn the ropes	v.) acquire special knowledge of a job
a breeze	n.) easy
cut out	adj.) suited to, have talent for

Exercise I. *Complete the sentences with the correct idiom.*
a) give me a break   b) works his fingers to the bone   c) pulling my leg   d) cut out   e) looking up
f) learn the ropes   g) get into the swing of things   h) a breeze   i) took on

1. I started a new job today. Now I have to _____.
2. He loves math and building things. He was _____ to be an engineer.
3. When you move into a new area, it is difficult to _____.
4. Science is so difficult for you but for me it's easy. It's _____.
5. I have enough money, a good job, a lot of friends. Things are _____ for me.
6. I need this job so badly. I will work very hard and stay overtime. Please _____.
7. I don't believe you're getting married next week. You're _____.
8. He's the hardest worker I know. He _____.
9. She goes to school; but she just _____ a part-time job, too.

Exercise II. *Rewrite the phrases in italics, using the proper idiomatic expression.*
1. I promise I'll study harder for the exam next time. Please *give me another chance.*
2. Stop *teasing me.*
3. I can do that. It's *easy.*
4. He had a difficult time last year but now everything's *improving.*
5. He just moved to town so he'll have to *learn about the area.*
6. He *works very hard.*
7. She loves to tell stories to little children. I think she's *suited* to be a teacher.
8. Whenever you start a new job, it's necessary to *learn all about it.*
9. He is a good dentist, but he's not *accepting* any more patients now.

Lesson 21.   A Hustler

Dialogue
Pat: He's pretty **sharp** when it comes to **feathering his own nest.**
Bob: He's a **hustler** who's out to make a **fast buck.** And he makes it **hand over fist.**
Pat: He'll try to **put the bite on** you by telling you a **cock and bull story.**
Bob: He has **a snowball's chance in hell.** I'm not a **soft touch.**

Vocabulary

sharp	adj.) smart, witty, quick-thinking
feather one's nest	v.) obtain extra money, often dishonestly, through one's job or position
hustler	n.) person who gets money aggressively or unethically
fast buck	n.) money obtained easily and often unethically
hand over fist	adv.) rapidly
put the bite on someone	v.) ask for a loan of money
cock and bull story	n.) an exaggerated or false story
a snowball's chance in hell	n.) no chance at all
soft touch	n.) one who gives money easily when asked

Exercise I. *Complete the sentences with the correct idiom.*
a) a cock and bull story   b) hand over fist   c) put the bite on   d) fast buck   e) feather his own nest
f) hustler   g) a snowball's chance in hell   h) a soft touch i) sharp

1. I can get some money easily. My dad's _____.
2. He's not going to tell me the truth. He'll make up _____.
3. He won't work. If he needs money, he'll _____ someone.
4. He has some very good ideas. You'll be surprised how _____ he is.
5. He'll always make money. He's a _____.
6. Everybody wants that item. If you sell it, you can make money _____.
7. He's always looking to make a _____.
8. That politician is dishonest. He's out to _____.
9. Do you think you're going to win the million dollar lottery? You don't have _____.

Exercise II. *Rewrite the phrases in italics, using the proper idiomatic expression.*
1. *He'll lend you a few dollars if you ask him.*
2. That's *an elaborate but false excuse.*
3. During the war, a lot of people made money *very quickly.*
4. He's a *very aggressive salesman.*
5. He's very *quick-thinking.*
6. He has *no chance at all.*
7. Be careful. He's going to *ask you for some money.*
8. He likes to make *money very easily.*
9. He *makes sure he benefits from any business deal.*

Lesson 22.   High Off the Hog

Dialogue

Grace: Someday you'll be **living high off the hog** but right now I know you're **strapped**.

Kay: Don't worry. I'll **land on my feet**.

Grace: You're always **in there pitching**. You don't **let any grass grow under your feet**.

Kay: That's true. Even if a job's **not so hot**, I'll **take a crack at it**.

Grace: I know. You've worked in a **sweatshop** and now you're **slinging hash**.

Vocabulary

live high off the hog	v.) have many luxuries, be very comfortable
strapped	adj.) having no money available
land on one's feet	v.) come out of a bad situation successfully
in there pitching	adj.) making an effort, trying
let grass grow under one's feet (neg.)	v.) waste time, be lazy
not so hot	adj.) not very good
take a crack at	v.) try, attempt
sweatshop	n.) a factory that has poor conditions, long hours, low pay
sling hash	v.) be a waitress

Exercise I. *Complete the sentences with the correct idiom.*

a) not so hot   b) sweatshop   c) let any grass grow under her feet   d) slinging hash   e) land on his feet
f) take a crack at   g) living high off the hog   h) strapped   i) in there pitching

1. She has four children, works full-time, and is active in politics. She doesn't _____.
2. If you can't understand that problem, let me _____ it.
3. Jane helped pay for some of her college expenses by working in a diner _____.
4. I know it's not easy getting a job. At least you are _____.
5. Even though he's having a difficult time financially, he will work it out and _____.
6. Before they won the lottery, they didn't have much money. Now they are _____.
7. His wife just had a baby. I wouldn't ask him to lend me money now. He's probably _____.
8. They told me the new restaurant had delicious food but the place is really _____.
9. When he first came to this country, he found it difficult getting a job. He took a job in a factory where the conditions were poor. It was a _____.

Exercise II. *Rewrite the phrases in italics, using the proper idiomatic expression.*

1. They *spend a lot of money and live very well.*
2. That factory *has poor working conditions.*
3. She's *a waitress.*
4. *He doesn't have any money right now.*
5. He may be having a little trouble now, but he'll *be successful.*
6. He goes from one project to another. He doesn't *waste any time.*
7. *If he doesn't succeed, he'll try again.*
8. That movie was *pretty bad.*
9. That subject is difficult, but he'll *attempt to learn it.*

Lesson 23.   Getting Down to Brass Tacks

Dialogue
Terry: Let's **get down to brass tacks.**
Marty: I'm **game.** I don't want to hear about this project in **dribs and drabs.** Let's get to the **nitty-gritty.**
Terry: I don't know what you have **up your sleeve** now, but your last idea was **out of this world.**
Marty: If we **sink our teeth** into the next project, we'll be **on the gravy train.**

Vocabulary

get down to brass tacks	v.) begin important work or business
game	adj.) willing, ready
dribs and drabs	n.) small quantities, little by little
nitty-gritty	n.) the essence or important part
have something up one's sleeve	v.) keep secretly ready for the right time
out of this world	adj.) wonderful, terrific
sink one's teeth into	v.) go to work seriously
on the gravy train	adj.) making a lot of money

Exercise I. *Complete the sentences with the correct idiom.*
a) nitty-gritty   b) sink your teeth into   c) out of this world   d) I'm game   e) on the gravy train
f) in dribs and drabs   g) has up his sleeve   h) get down to brass tacks

1. You want to make plans to go to Japan next year. Okay, _____.
2. Stop talking on the phone. We have to discuss business. Let's _____.
3. Tell me all about the party now. I don't want to hear it _____.
4. Tell me what's really bothering you. Let's get down to the _____.
5. He's planning something special. They have been talking secretly for hours. I'd like to know what he _____.
6. That dinner was delicious. It was _____.
7. When recording artists sell a million records, they are _____.
8. If you're going to pass that course, you better _____ those books.

Exercise II. *Rewrite the phrases in italics, using the proper idiomatic expression.*
1. *He won the lottery.*
2. That's *terrific.*
3. Just tell me the *important part.*
4. That sounds like a good idea. *I'll go along with it.*
5. Let's *start to discuss business.*
6. I'm getting this work done *little by little.*
7. *He's hiding something.*
8. That project is due. Let's *seriously go to work on* it.

Lesson 24.   Straight from the Horse's Mouth

Dialogue
Artie: How did you **get wind of** that terrific business deal?
Jason: I got it **straight from the horse's mouth** and I'd like to **get in on the ground floor.**
Artie: I hope nobody **beats you to the punch.** Maybe we should both **jump on the bandwagon.**
Jason: Do you think we'll **clean up?**
Artie: I'm sure we'll make a **pretty penny.**

Vocabulary

get wind of	v.) find out, hear gossip or rumors about
straight from the horse's mouth	adv.) directly from the person involved
get in on the ground floor	v.) start from the beginning so you'll have full advantage of any favorable outcome
beat someone to the punch (draw)	v.) do something before someone else can
jump (get) (climb) on the band-wagon	v.) join a popular activity
clean up	v.) make a big profit
pretty penny	n.) a lot of money

Exercise I. *Complete the sentences with the correct idiom.*
a) straight from the horse's mouth   b) beat everyone to the punch   c) cleaning up   d) get in on the ground floor   e) got wind of   f) a pretty penny   g) got on the bandwagon

1. That's a beautiful sports car. I'm sure it costs _____.
2. Let's be the first to sign up for the cruise to Bermuda. We'll _____.
3. That information is definitely true. I got it _____.
4. They made a lot of money investing in that company. Too bad I _____ it too late.
5. He invested money when that stock was very low. Now it has tripled and he's _____.
6. After everyone decided to vacation in the mountains, John also _____.
7. The area hasn't been developed yet. If you buy land now, you'll _____.

Exercise II. *Rewrite the phrases in italics, using the proper idiomatic expression.*
1. The police *heard rumors that there was going to be* a bank robbery.
2. That designer dress cost *a lot of money.*
3. He decided to *join that group* just when it was getting popular.
4. I heard the news *directly from him.*
5. I would like to *start from the beginning* so that we can make a good profit.
6. I don't want anyone to *start before me.*
7. He *made a lot of money* in the stock market.

Lesson 25.   Coming Through with Flying Colors

Dialogue
Jack: Were you **a drop out?**
Hank: **Sort of. I kidded around** too much. When I saw I wasn't **getting to first base,** I **cut out.**
Jack: Well, you **came through with flying colors** on this test. You didn't **miss the boat.**
Hank: Thanks. I knew I had to **take the bull by the horns.**
Jack: You deserve **a pat on the back.**

Vocabulary

a drop out	n.) one who doesn't complete a study course
sort of	adv.) almost, not quite; like, similar to; rather
kid around	v.) fool, play, joke
get to first base	v.) make a good start, succeed, make progress
cut out	v.) leave
come through (pass) with flying colors	v.) succeed, win, exceed
miss the boat	v.) lose an opportunity
take the bull by the horns	v.) take strong action
a pat on the back	n.) praise

Exercise I. *Complete the sentences with the correct idiom.*
a) came through with flying colors   b) sort of   c) drop out   d) missed the boat   e) get to first base
f) take the bull by the horns   g) kid around   h) a pat on the back   i) cut out

1. It's too bad he didn't finish school. Why was he a _____?
2. I tried to impress her, but I couldn't _____.
3. You never tasted turkey? It's _____ like chicken.
4. He studied hard and got all A's. Give him _____.
5. That class is a lot of fun. They learn English while they _____.
6. He studied very hard for that exam. When he got his grades, he was happy to see he

   _____.

7. He needs more money, so he is going to _____ and ask for a raise.
8. If I bought a lot of gold at $35 an ounce, I would have a great deal of money. I _____.
9. He didn't like the party so he _____ early.

Exercise II. *Rewrite the phrases in italics, using the proper idiomatic expression.*
1. He *never completed high school.*
2. *I did very well on that examination.*
3. In order to stop crime, we're going to have to *take strong action.*
4. When you're being interviewed for a job, that's the time to *make a good impression.*
5. Should I invest in that company? I don't want to *lose a good opportunity.*
6. That was a good job. You deserve *a lot of praise.*
7. If we're not busy at work today, I'm going to *leave* early.
8. I wouldn't say she was beautiful, but she is *rather* pretty.
9. I didn't mean to say that. I was only *fooling.*

Lesson 26. The Black Sheep

Dialogue

Dan: Why are you **taking your hat off to me?**
Frank: Because you succeeded even though you **had two strikes against you.** You were born on **the wrong side of the tracks** and you were the **black sheep** of the family **to boot.**
Dan: Well, I **came a long way** mainly because I was a **go-getter.**
Frank: You also **have a head on your shoulders.** I'm glad to see you're **batting a thousand.**

Vocabulary

take one's hat off to someone	v.) admire, respect, praise
have two strikes against one	v.) be in a difficult situation with little chance of success
the wrong side of the tracks	n.) the poor section of town, implying social inferiority
black sheep	n.) a family member with a bad reputation
to boot	adv.) in addition, also
come a long way	v.) make great progress
go-getter	n.) ambitious person
have a head on one's shoulders	v.) be smart or sensible
bat a thousand	v.) have a perfect record, whether good or bad

Exercise I. *Complete the sentences with the correct idiom.*

a) take your hat off to him   b) has a head on his shoulders   c) go-getter   d) from the wrong side of the tracks   e) come a long way   f) to boot   g) has two strikes against him   h) black sheep   i) batting a thousand

1. His brother is a doctor, his sister is a teacher, but he just got sent to jail. He's the _____.
2. He's always busy working. He's a _____.
3. He's had a crippling disease since childhood but he finished college and became a lawyer. You have to _____.
4. He can figure out complicated math problems very quickly. He _____.
5. I was able to win every game today. I'm _____.
6. Bettina was very shy but now she talks with confidence. She's _____.
7. She comes from a wealthy family. Her parents did not want her to marry anyone _____.
8. He wanted that job but he can't write well and he's had little experience. He _____.
9. She's gaining weight, so I was surprised she ordered macaroni and chocolate ice cream _____.

Exercise II. *Rewrite the phrases in italics, using the proper idiomatic expression.*

1. He is the *only one in his family who has a bad reputation.*
2. I *was perfect* on the test—I failed every question.
3. He's a *very ambitious person.*
4. He's *made a lot of progress* in his life.
5. Not only is he stupid but he's ugly. *I don't think he'll be successful.*
6. He is a wonderful person. You have to *respect and admire him.*
7. His family *was poor and never socialized with the rich.*
8. He *is a very intelligent person.*
9. He is not only a lawyer, but a teacher *also.*

Lesson 27.   In a Jam

Dialogue

Doug: I hear you're **in a jam.**

Larry: I want to **get out of** an agreement with that **fly-by-night** organization. I don't think they're **on the level.**

Doug: You should have **double-checked** before you put your **John Hancock** on the contract. Now your company will **end up** financially **in the red.**

Larry: I guess I'll have to **chalk it up** to experience.

Vocabulary

in a jam	adj.) in trouble
get out of	v.) withdraw
fly-by-night	adj.) unreliable, untrustworthy
on the level	adj.) honest
double-check	v.) reinvestigate thoroughly, look again for errors
John Hancock	n.) signature
end up	v.) finish
in the red	adv. or adj.) losing money
chalk up	v.) record, score

Exercise I. *Complete the sentences with the correct idiom.*

a) John Hancock   b) get out of   c) in a jam   d) chalked up   e) double-check   f) on the level   g) in the red   h) fly-by-night   i) end up

1. I'm always getting in trouble. Why am I always _____?
2. I don't trust that company. I think they're a _____ organization.
3. They're not telling you the whole story. I don't think they're _____.
4. They want my _____ on that contract.
5. I heard he raced in the marathon. How did he _____?
6. I don't remember locking the door. Let me _____.
7. They're getting married next month but she doesn't really love him. I think she'll _____ it.
8. That company keeps losing money. It's _____.
9. She studied hard this year and _____ some good grades.

Exercise II. *Rewrite the phrases in italics, using the proper idiomatic expression.*

1. Put your *signature* right here.
2. It doesn't sound *honest* to me.
3. Don't try to *cancel* your doctor's appointment.
4. *They keep losing money.*
5. *That company is new and has a bad reputation.*
6. Are you sure that's the right amount? Let's *look again.*
7. That new team *won* another victory.
8. I'm *in trouble.*
9. You worked very hard in that course. How did you *finish?*

Lesson 28. On the Go

Dialogue

Josh: That trip was **murder**. I'm **beat**.
Lucy: Why don't you **grab 40 winks**?
Josh: I think I will. I've been **on the go** constantly. They **ran us ragged**.
Lucy: Did you go sightseeing?
Josh: Yes. We were **roped into** a tour, but it was **for the birds**. And we **paid through the nose**.
Lucy: It sounds like they **took you for a ride** in more ways than one.

Vocabulary

murder	n.) a difficult or painful ordeal
beat	adj.) tired, exhausted
grab 40 winks	v.) take a nap
on the go	adj.) busy running around
run ragged	v.) tire, exhaust
rope into	v.) trick, persuade, or pressure
for the birds	adj.) terrible, awful
pay through the nose	v.) pay too much
take someone for a ride	v.) cheat, swindle

Exercise I. *Complete the sentences with the correct idiom.*

a) ran ourselves ragged   b) grab 40 winks   c) pay through the nose   d) murder   e) was taken for a ride   f) beat   g) roped into   h) on the go   i) for the birds

1. After I eat dinner, I feel sleepy. I like to _____.
2. I didn't like that movie. It was _____.
3. I was looking for that toy for a long time. I finally found it even though I had to _____.
4. I worked so hard today. I'm _____.
5. You can never find her at home. She's always _____.
6. After he bought a diamond ring, he found out it was only glass. He _____.
7. I'm the only one who works overtime. How did I ever get _____ this?
8. We went shopping today. I'm so tired. We _____.
9. She gets very bad headaches. They are really _____.

Exercise II. *Rewrite the phrases in italics, using the proper idiomatic expression.*

1. I'm *tired*.
2. That chemistry class is *very difficult*.
3. That man is not honest. He'll *cheat* you if he can.
4. That restaurant was *awful*.
5. I was watching my sister's baby today. He *tired me out*.
6. He works, goes to school and has a girlfriend. He's *so busy*.
7. I don't feel well. Maybe I'll *take a nap*.
8. He didn't want to do it but he was *tricked into* it.
9. Don't buy groceries in that supermarket. You'll *pay more than they're worth*.

Lesson 29.   Raising Cain

Dialogue
Mark: My vacation plans **fell through.** My wife's going to **raise Cain.**
Tony: Don't **let on** to her yet. Maybe everything will **turn out** okay.
Mark: I hope so. I hate to **back out of** a promise. I know my wife **had her heart set on** it.
Tony: If you can't go, **make it up** to her. She'll forgive you. She won't **hold a grudge.**

Vocabulary

fall through	v.) fail, collapse
raise Cain	v.) create a disturbance, make trouble
let on	v.) reveal, inform, tell
turn out	v.) result, end
back out of	v.) withdraw, end an obligation or promise
have one's heart set on	v.) desire greatly
make it up to someone	v.) compensate for an unfulfilled promise or debt
hold a grudge	v.) not forgive someone for an insult or injury

Exercise I. *Complete the sentences with the correct idiom.*
a) fell through   b) holds a grudge   c) heart set on   d) turn out   e) back out of   f) let on   g) make it up to   h) raised Cain

1. I have a dentist's appointment but my tooth feels better now. I think I'll _____ it.
2. He was going to go to college but his father died. Now he has to go to work and support his family. All his plans _____.
3. She just found out she was having a baby. She doesn't want to _____ to anyone yet.
4. I'm sorry I didn't come home for dinner but I'll _____ you. Next week I'll take you to a terrific restaurant.
5. She will never speak to her again. She _____.
6. She is very excited about her vacation. She's had her _____ going to Japan.
7. How did the baseball game _____?
8. When his teenage son took the family car without permission, the father _____.

Exercise II. *Rewrite the phrases in italics, using the proper idiomatic expression.*
1. Don't *be angry at a mistake I made a long time ago.*
2. Did you *reveal* that you knew any important information?
3. My dreams of the future *collapsed.*
4. When his son brought home a bad report from school, the father *created a commotion* at the dinner table.
5. Don't *withdraw from* any promise made at the meeting.
6. *He had a great desire to return* to his country.
7. It's raining. We can't go to the beach. *In exchange,* I'll take you to a movie.
8. *What were the results of your speech?*

Lesson 30. Behind the 8-Ball

Dialogue
Chris: I'm **behind the 8-ball.**
Ben: What did you do wrong now?
Chris: I have so much work. I can't **make a dent in** it.
Ben: Maybe if you'd **buckle down,** you wouldn't be **up to your ears** in work.
Chris: My job is **no bed of roses** and my boss is **off his rocker.**
Ben: You'd better **watch your P's and Q's** before you get **canned.**

Vocabulary

behind the 8-ball	adj.) in trouble
make a dent in	v.) make progress
buckle down	v.) study or work very hard
up to one's ears	adj.) deeply immersed in
no bed of roses	n.) uncomfortable, unhappy situation
off one's rocker	adj.) crazy
watch (mind) one's P's and Q's	v.) act very carefully, pay attention to details
can	v.) fire, dismiss

Exercise I. *Complete the sentences with the correct idiom.*

a) off your rocker   b) make a dent in   c) up to my ears   d) buckle down   e) canned   f) mind your P's and Q's   g) no bed of roses   h) behind the 8-ball

1. If you're having dinner with your boss, you have to _____.
2. Every day he took a two-hour lunch. The boss _____ him.
3. Being married to a policeman is _____.
4. He didn't get his wife a birthday present. He is _____.
5. If you think I'm going to loan you $1,000 to take a vacation, you're _____.
6. I'm trying to finish up my work but they keep giving me more. I can't _____ it.
7. If you want to learn English, you have to _____.
8. In the winter, I'm not so busy, but during the summer, I'm _____ in work.

Exercise II. *Rewrite the phrases in italics, using the proper idiomatic expression.*
1. I'm *so busy at* work.
2. Being a waitress is *not the easiest job in the world.*
3. I have to *study very hard.*
4. He's *fired.*
5. He didn't *make any progress in* cleaning up his desk.
6. *Act very carefully and have good manners* when you are at the office meeting.
7. He's *crazy.*
8. If I don't get this report out tonight, I'll be *in trouble.*

Lesson 31. Jack-of-All-Trades

Dialogue
Chuck: He's a **jack-of-all-trades** and **top-notch** in every one.
Dan: Really? He looks like a **bum** who's been **drowning his sorrows** in **sleazy dives.**
Chuck: Nope. He's really a **high-brow** but he had a couple of **tough breaks** and **hit the skids.**

Vocabulary
jack-of-all-trades	n.) person who can do many kinds of work
top-notch	adj.) excellent, the best
bum	n.) worthless person
drown one's sorrows	v.) drink liquor to forget unhappiness
sleazy	adj.) shoddy, dirty, in poor condition
dive	n.) a disreputable, low-class bar or nightclub
high-brow	n.) intellectual, cultured person
tough break	n.) unlucky event, misfortune
hit the skids	v.) come upon bad times

Exercise I. *Complete the sentences with the correct idiom.*
a) tough breaks   b) hit the skids   c) top-notch   d) high-brow   e) sleazy   f) drown his sorrows
g) jack-of-all-trades   h) bum   i) dive

1. I didn't realize he was so intelligent. He didn't appear to be a _____.
2. That's one of the best organizations in the country. It's really _____.
3. He doesn't do anything all day long. He's totally useless. He's a _____.
4. A lot of unfortunate things have been happening to him lately. It's too bad he's had so many
   _____.
5. At one time he had a lot of money but he lost it in the stock market. After that, he
   _____.
6. I wouldn't go into that bar to make a phone call. It looks like a _____.
7. He's been very unhappy lately. I hope he doesn't start drinking to _____.
8. Ask Ed to help you. He can fix anything. He's a _____.
9. That used to be a good neighborhood but now you would be disgusted to walk down the street. The
   area is _____.

Exercise II. *Rewrite the phrases in italics, using the proper idiomatic expression.*
1. That's *an excellent* restaurant.
2. He never works. *He's worthless.*
3. Their neighborhood used to be nice but now it's *run down and dirty.*
4. That *nightclub* attracts very disreputable people.
5. It's a shame that he *came upon such bad times.*
6. He's *an intellectual.*
7. He's had a lot of *bad luck.*
8. He's drinking *because he's unhappy.*
9. John is *skilled enough to do any job in the company.*

Lesson 32.   Out on a Limb

Dialogue
Mike: **The coast is clear.** Let's **give him the slip.**
Rob: **My heart is in my mouth.**
Mike: You'd better **wash your hands of** this affair before you're put **in the klink.**
Rob: You're right. If he **blabs,** I'm **out on a limb.**
Mike: Why do you always **stick your neck out?**

Vocabulary

The coast is clear.	No enemy is in sight.
give someone the slip	v.) escape, get away from
One's heart is in one's mouth.	One is nervous, fearful, or anxious.
wash one's hands of	v.) refuse responsibility for, abandon
in the klink	adj.) in jail
blab	v.) talk too much
out on a limb	adj. or adv.) in a dangerous, exposed position; one's ideas are openly known
stick one's neck out	v.) look for trouble, take risks

Exercise I. *Complete the sentences with the correct idiom.*
a) the coast is clear   b) my heart is in my mouth   c) wash your hands of him   d) stick my neck out
e) out on a limb   f) give them the slip   g) blabbing   h) in the klink

1. The bank robbers weren't caught by the police. Did they _____?
2. I'm speaking before 200 people tonight. _____.
3. If he lies or hurts you, you should _____.
4. If you commit a crime, you'll be put _____.
5. I want it quiet when I'm watching TV but my children are usually _____.
6. Nobody is around. We can leave. _____.
7. Whenever I help somebody, I get in trouble. I should never _____.
8. By speaking up against her boss, she's put herself _____.

Exercise II. *Rewrite the phrases in italics, using the proper idiomatic expression.*
1. He's always *looking for trouble.*
2. *I don't see anybody who would stop us.*
3. Let's *get rid of him.*
4. I can't believe he's *in jail.*
5. She's always *talking.*
6. I didn't realize I was putting myself *in a dangerous position.*
7. Traffic was so bad on the way to the airport, that I thought I would miss my plane. *I was so nervous.*
8. That's not your responsibility. *Don't get involved.*

Lesson 33.   Twiddling One's Thumbs

Dialogue
Dawn: I hate to **break the news** to you but I'm **calling it quits.**
Jeremy: I see you're **beside yourself,** but don't **throw in the towel.**
Dawn: I have to. Sales have **fallen off** and I'm sitting around **twiddling my thumbs.** Business **stinks.**
Jeremy: The **bottom line** is that stores like yours are **a dime a dozen.**

Vocabulary
break the news	v.) tell a surprising fact
call it quits	v.) stop, finish, quit
be beside one's self	v.) be very upset, nervous, frantic
throw in the towel	v.) surrender, give up
fall off (drop off)	v.) decrease
twiddle one's thumbs	v.) not busy, not working
stink	v.) to be of extremely bad quality, to be terrible
bottom line	n.) end result, ultimate cause, deciding factor
a dime a dozen	n.) common, easily obtained

Exercise I. *Complete the sentences with the correct idiom.*
a) beside herself   b) fell off   c) a dime a dozen   d) threw in the towel   e) stinks   f) the bottom line
g) call it quits   h) twiddle her thumbs   i) break the news

1. It is difficult to _____ that a loved one has died.
2. After many years of an unhappy marriage, they decided to _____.
3. When the mother could not find her child, she was _____.
4. The salesgirls were not as busy after the holidays because business _____.
5. She won the lottery. Now she can stay home and _____.
6. She never tried hard. She always _____.
7. He never studied in school and _____ is, he can't read well.
8. In Hollywood, pretty girls are _____.
9. That movie is awful. It _____.

Exercise II. *Rewrite the phrases in italics, using the proper idiomatic expression.*
1. It's not easy finding teachers today, but years ago they were *easily obtained.*
2. Studying to be a doctor was too hard. He *gave up.*
3. Tourist travel to Florida *decreases* during the summer months.
4. He no longer wants to act. *He's ending his career.*
5. I was surprised when she *told me* they were getting married.
6. He failed his history class and is *very upset.*
7. She quit her job and now she *doesn't do anything.*
8. This product may be imperfect, *but what do the sales figures say?*
9. He's always depressed. He thinks his whole life *is terrible.*

Lesson 34. Play It by Ear

Dialogue
Don: He **butted in** and **loused up** the deal.
Scott: Don't worry. We'll **iron out** the problems. Just **play it by ear.**
Don: Do you think we'll still get our **foot in the door?**
Scott: Only if we **handle them with kid gloves.** We don't want to **get the brush-off.**
Don: I'll **make sure** he doesn't **put his foot in his mouth** again.

Vocabulary

butt in	v.) interfere
louse up	v.) ruin
iron out	v.) work out
play it by ear	v.) make your decision according to the situation
foot in the door	n.) opening; hopeful beginning of success
handle with kid gloves	v.) be very careful, tactful
get the brush-off	v.) be ignored or dismissed
make sure	v.) see about something yourself, check
put one's foot in one's mouth	v.) speak carelessly, make a rude or insensitive comment

Exercise I. *Complete the sentences with the correct idiom.*
a) iron it out   b) play it by ear   c) loused it up   d) handle them with kid gloves   e) the brush-off
f) foot in the door   g) puts his foot in it   h) butt in   i) make sure

1. Before I go out, I _____ I have my keys and money.
2. They're very sensitive people. You have to _____.
3. He doesn't think of what he's saying and usually _____.
4. When two people are arguing, you should not _____.
5. They had a big fight, but now they want to _____.
6. She didn't want to speak to him, so she gave him _____.
7. She asked me to type the letter for her. I made so many mistakes. I _____.
8. That company won't give me any business. Maybe if I take their executives out to dinner, I'll get my _____.
9. I'm not sure we should tell them our plans. We'll have to _____.

Exercise II. *Rewrite the phrases in italics, using the proper idiomatic expression.*
1. You have to *be very careful what you say to her.*
2. Try to *work out* your differences.
3. Don't *ruin my plans.*
4. Please don't *interfere with* my life.
5. If I'm granted an interview for that job, *it's the only opening I'll need.*
6. Don't speak carelessly because you may *hurt someone.*
7. *They ignored me.*
8. *Wait until you find out what's happening before you decide what to do.*
9. Before you leave the house, *check* that the door is locked.

Lesson 35. Off the Top of One's Head

Dialogue
Cynthia: I looked over this place **with a fine-tooth comb.** I can't find the notes for my speech.
Tommy: Don't **knock yourself out** looking for them. I'm sure you can **wing it.**
Cynthia: I don't know about that. I'm **sweating bullets.** I don't **have a prayer.**
Tommy: It's **a snap.** Do it **off the top of your head.**
Cynthia: I know I'm going to **blow it.**
Tommy: No you won't. You can **pull it off.**

Vocabulary
with a fine-tooth comb	adv.) very carefully
knock oneself out	v.) make a great effort
wing it	v.) rely only on one's knowledge; act without preparation
sweat bullets	v.) be nervous; be very hot
have a prayer (neg.)	v.) have a chance
a snap	n.) an easy task
off the top of one's head	adv.) from memory, spontaneously
blow it	v.) lose a chance, make a mistake, forget
pull something off	v.) accomplish something remarkable

Exercise I. *Complete the sentences with the correct idiom.*
a) fine-tooth comb   b) off the top of my head   c) wing it   d) blew it   e) pull it off   f) knocked herself out   g) sweating bullets   h) a snap   i) has a prayer

1. He's so nervous. He's _____.
2. He wasn't prepared for that job interview. He knew he _____.
3. She invited 20 people for dinner and she _____.
4. Somebody robbed him. The detectives went over his apartment with a _____.
5. That teacher is not strict. Getting a good grade in her class is _____.
6. I can't think of his address _____.
7. If you're not prepared, it's sometimes very difficult to _____.
8. Many other people have tried to win the contest. I hope I can _____.
9. She wants to pass the test, but she didn't study. I don't think she _____.

Exercise II. *Rewrite the phrases in italics, using the proper idiomatic expression.*
1. Despite a lot of problems, she finished college. She *accomplished something remarkable.*
2. *Without studying,* I won't remember the answers.
3. I'm *incredibly hot* today.
4. I *really tried* to make this a great party.
5. You don't have *a chance.*
6. *He looked everywhere in the apartment* for his car keys.
7. I didn't study for that test, so I will have to *rely on my own knowledge.*
8. That test was *very easy.*
9. In the middle of the speech, she *forgot her lines.*

Lesson 36.   The Rat Race

Dialogue

Sarah: This **rat race** is **getting me down.** I'm **at the end of my rope.**
Zachary: Don't **come apart at the seams.** Look for another job.
Sarah: I always get **cold feet.** I'll be in this **dead-end job** 'til I **kick the bucket.**
Zachary: Don't **sell yourself short.** Maybe your boss will give you a promotion. Tell him you want
           to **talk turkey.**

Vocabulary

rat race	n.) endless, competitive striving; hurried, material existence
get one down	v.) depress
at the end of one's rope	adj.) desperate, with nowhere to turn
come apart at the seams	v.) be upset and lose control
get cold feet	v.) be afraid at the last minute, lose confidence
dead-end job	n.) position with no future
kick the bucket	v.) die
sell oneself short	v.) underestimate oneself
talk turkey	v.) discuss seriously, in a business-like manner

Exercise I. *Complete the sentences with the correct idiom.*

a) talk turkey   b) came apart at the seams   c) kicked the bucket   d) rat race   e) cold feet   f) at the
end of his rope   g) sell yourself short   h) dead-end job   i) getting me down

1. I was going to jump from an airplane with a parachute, but I got_____.
2. All he does is work, work, work, spend, spend, spend. His life is a _____.
3. He lived to be 100 years old, then he _____.
4. If you're really serious about buying my car, let's _____.
5. He looked everywhere for a job and he can't find one. He's _____.
6. Every day we've had rain. It's been _____.
7. He won't become an executive in that company. He has a _____.
8. You're very smart. You can do that job. You shouldn't _____.
9. When her husband died, she _____.

Exercise II. *Rewrite the phrases in italics, using the proper idiomatic expression.*

1. I was surprised to hear *he died.*
2. I want to *speak seriously.*
3. *That type of life has no purpose.*
4. *He doesn't know where to go for help.*
5. Not having a vacation this year is *very depressing.*
6. When they took her child to the hospital, she *went out of control.*
7. You're a good worker. Don't *underestimate yourself.*
8. *I'll never be promoted in this company.*
9. He'll never get married. *He'll get scared.*

Lesson 37. Keyed Up

Dialogue

Brett: He's **hyper** lately. I don't know why he's so **keyed up**.

Ron: I think he **bit off more than he could chew** when he took this job. He doesn't **know if he's coming or going**.

Brett: He keeps **running around in circles**. He better **simmer down** and **get a grip on himself**.

Ron: It's too late. Frankly, I think he's already **lost his marbles**.

Vocabulary

hyper	adj.) very energetic, anxious, unable to sit still
keyed up	adj.) tense, anxious, nervous
bite off more than one can chew	v.) try to do more than one can physically or mentally handle
know if one is coming or going (neg.)	v.) be able to think clearly, know what to do
run around in circles	v.) act confused, do a lot but accomplish little
simmer down	v.) become calm, quiet
get a grip on oneself	v.) take control of one's feelings
lose one's marbles	v.) go insane, act irrationally

Exercise I. *Complete the sentences with the correct idiom.*

a) running around in circles   b) bit off more than he could chew   c) keyed up   d) know if he's coming or going   e) lost his marbles   f) hyper   g) simmer down   h) get a grip on herself

1. If he gets too upset, try to have him _____.
2. Anyone who insults his boss has _____.
3. Her child doesn't sit still. He's so _____.
4. He works six days a week and goes to school part-time. I think he _____.
5. His wife just had a baby. He's so excited he doesn't _____.
6. When she heard her child was in an accident, she tried to _____ after her initial panic.
7. Before his job interview, he was _____.
8. She lost her child in the supermarket. No matter how hard she looked, she couldn't find him. She was _____.

Exercise II. *Rewrite the phrases in italics, using the proper idiomatic expression.*

1. He is so busy, he *can't think clearly*.
2. Before an examination, he's *very tense*.
3. He *went insane*.
4. You're too excited. *Calm down.*
5. *He can't sit still.*
6. *He can't do everything he promised.*
7. She's *going from one place to the other but she's not getting anything done*.
8. When he heard the bad news he had to *control his feelings*.

Lesson 38. Pounding the Pavement

Dialogue

Jay: John's going to be **pounding the pavement** if he doesn't stop **shooting the breeze** all day.

Kay: He's starting to **get under the boss's skin**. He is **up to here with** John.

Jay: I hope the boss doesn't put me **on the spot** about John. He'll probably give me **the third degree**.

Kay: I know you don't **have the heart** to **squeal** on him but I think you have to **come clean**.

Vocabulary

pound the pavement	v.) look for a job
shoot the breeze	v.) talk idly or gossip
get under someone's skin	v.) annoy, bother, upset
up to here with	adj.) disgusted with another's continual behavior
on the spot	adj. or adv.) in a difficult or embarrassing situation
the third degree	n.) prolonged questioning
squeal	v.) inform
have the heart to (neg.)	v.) be pitiless or thoughtless enough
come clean	v.) tell the truth

Exercise I. *Complete the sentences with the correct idiom.*

a) shoot the breeze   b) pounding the pavement   c) up to here with   d) squealed   e) on the spot
f) the third degree   g) came clean   h) get under my skin   i) have the heart to

1. Work is difficult to find. He's been _____ for a week.
2. I just cashed my paycheck, so when he asked me to lend him some money, I was _____.
3. All his friends wanted to know about his exciting evening. As soon as he came in the door, they gave him _____.
4. Jane ate the cookies. The mother asked the children who ate them, but nobody _____.
5. The criminal confessed. Everybody was surprised he _____.
6. I call up my girlfriend every night and we _____.
7. Some TV commercials _____.
8. My telephone bills are so high. I'm _____ them.
9. She studied so hard that I don't _____ tell her she failed.

Exercise II. *Rewrite the phrases in italics, using the proper idiomatic expression.*

1. The police *questioned him for a long time.*
2. Finally he *informed* on his friends.
3. I was *in a difficult situation.*
4. He was *out looking for a job.*
5. He enjoys *talking with people.*
6. Crying children *bother me.*
7. The mother asked her child where he got the candy. He better *tell the truth.*
8. My car is giving me trouble. I'm *disgusted with* it.
9. *I'm not thoughtless enough to* tell her I saw her boyfriend with another woman.

Lesson 39.   A Hard Nut to Crack

Dialogue
Matt: I can't **put my finger on** why business is bad. It's a **hard nut to crack.**
Shelley: Do you **go overboard** when you buy merchandise?
Matt: Sometimes I **get carried away** but I usually buy **within reason.**
Shelley: Let's try to **pinpoint** it. Is your rent too high?
Matt: What I pay would **make your hair stand on end.**
Shelley: If that's the problem, maybe you should **pull up stakes.**

Vocabulary
put one's finger on	v.) find precisely, remember exactly
go overboard	v.) overact, be reckless
carried away	adj.) adversely influenced by strong emotions
within reason	adv. or adj.) sensible, reasonable; reasonably
pinpoint	v.) find exact location or cause
hard (tough) nut to crack	n.) something difficult to do or understand
make one's hair stand on end	v.) frighten, horrify
pull up stakes	v.) move to another location

Exercise I. *Complete the sentences with the correct idiom.*
a) make your hair stand on end   b) within reason   c) carried away   d) pinpoint   e) put my finger on   f) go overboard   g) a hard nut to crack   h) pull up stakes

1. I haven't been feeling very well lately, but I can't _____ the cause.
2. Many executives get transferred and their families must _____.
3. Her cooking is so good, I always _____ and eat too much.
4. The movie was so sad, she started crying loudly. She didn't realize she got _____.
5. That's a beautiful dress. I'll buy it if the price is _____.
6. Getting into show business is _____.
7. The extreme poverty in that country would _____.
8. I know I met him somewhere but I can't _____ it.

Exercise II. *Rewrite the phrases in italics, using the proper idiomatic expression.*
1. The American pioneers kept *moving to another location.*
2. Passing chemistry courses in college is *difficult to do.*
3. Going in that old house at night would *frighten you.*
4. That's a beautiful watch. I'll buy it if the price is *sensible.*
5. Some dieters *don't use judgment* when eating.
6. When I went to Mexico, silver jewelry was so cheap. I *spent more than I wanted to.*
7. I know the author of that book but I just can't *remember* her name.
8. I can't *remember* the exact location.

Lesson 40.   Back to the Drawing Board

Dialogue

Andrew: I'm a **goner.** My new project **bombed.**

Louis: I thought it would **go over big** with the boss. Why did it **go up in smoke?**

Andrew: A problem arose **from left field,** and now I'm back to **square one.**

Louis: How much will it cost now? Can you give me a **ballpark figure?**

Andrew: I won't know for another week. Meantime, I have to get **back to the drawing board.**

Vocabulary

goner	n.) someone in a lot of trouble
bomb	v.) fail, be unsuccessful
go over big	v.) be very successful
go up in smoke	v.) disappear, fail to materialize
from left field	adv.) unexpectedly; with an odd or unclear connection to the subject
square one	n.) the beginning
ballpark figure	n.) approximate amount
back to the drawing board	adv.) ready to start over, refine or rethink an idea

Exercise I. *Complete the sentences with the correct idiom.*

a) up in smoke   b) from left field   c) back to the drawing board   d) bombed   e) goner   f) went over big   g) square one   h) ballpark figure

1. He was going to Europe, but his father got sick. His plans went _____.
2. I didn't study for that exam, and my future depends on it. I'm a _____.
3. She made a delicious meal for dinner. It _____.
4. We went to see that new play, but nobody likes it. It _____.
5. We were in the middle of a business meeting when, _____, he asked about the weather.
6. Despite all my research, I need a new subject. I'm back to _____.
7. How much does it cost to build a house? Give me a _____.
8. The boss wants new sales plans, so he sent us _____.

Exercise II. *Rewrite the phrases in italics, using the proper idiomatic expression.*

1. When his father sees his bad grades, he'll be *in trouble.*
2. This speech is not as good as it should be. I'll have to go *to work on it some more.*
3. Everyone thought the play would be good, but it *was terrible.*
4. I'm not sure how much a new car would cost. Give me *an estimate.*
5. He mentioned some new ideas at the meeting and *everyone liked them.*
6. Every time I try to assemble this toy, it's wrong. I keep going back to *the beginning.*
7. He wanted to be a lawyer, but since he couldn't get into law school, his plans *never materialized.*
8. I asked her for advice, but her ideas were *unrelated to my problems.*

Lesson 41. Passing the Buck

Dialogue
Dave: Did you **get up on the wrong side of the bed** this morning?
Gloria: No. I'm **out of sorts** because I can't find the **nincompoop** who **botched up** the report.
Dave: What happened?
Gloria: I asked for a **rough** estimate but it was way **off base.**
Dave: So now you can't **pin anyone down** because they're all **passing the buck.**
Gloria: Right. Next time I'll put everything **in black and white.**

Vocabulary

get up on the wrong side of the bed	v.) be in a bad mood
out of sorts	adj.) in a bad mood, irritable
nincompoop	n.) a stupid person, a fool
botch up	v.) make a big mistake, ruin
rough	adj.) approximate
off base	adj.) inaccurate
pin someone down	v.) make someone tell the truth or agree to something
pass the buck	v.) shift responsibility to others
in black and white	adj.) in writing

Exercise I. *Complete the sentences with the correct idiom.*
a) get up on the wrong side of the bed   b) in black and white   c) out of sorts   d) nincompoop
e) botched up   f) passing the buck   g) pin him down   h) off base   i) rough

1. Don't believe everything you see _____.
2. You are in a bad mood today. Did you _____?
3. He gets annoyed so quickly. I don't understand why he's _____.
4. He made a mistake on the payroll and _____ everyone's paycheck.
5. He doesn't know how to act well around people. He's a _____.
6. Do you think I only paid $100 for this gold necklace? You're way _____.
7. Nobody is claiming responsibility for their actions. They're all _____.
8. I know you're not sure when you can have the report ready, but give me a _____ idea.
9. He won't give you a direct answer unless you _____.

Exercise II. *Rewrite the phrases in italics, using the proper idiomatic expression.*
1. I don't want a verbal agreement. I want to see it *written.*
2. *He's in a bad mood.*
3. He *made some bad mistakes in his career.*
4. Why is he always *irritable?*
5. When will the project be finished? I need *an approximate* date.
6. I can't get the information I need. Everyone keeps *sending me to another department.*
7. When I asked him if I could buy a good fur coat for $500, he told me I was *far from the right cost.*
8. I don't want him helping us with the project because he is *a fool.*
9. She never gets a chance to see him unless she *makes him agree to* a date ahead of time.

Lesson 42.   A Song and Dance

Dialogue

Mark: Don't give me **a song and dance.** It's time you **stood on your own two feet.**

Phil: I **gave it my best shot** but any ideas I've had, you've **shot full of holes.**

Mark: Your ideas haven't been **up to par** lately. That's why I've **thrown cold water on them.**

Phil: I've been upset because I've been **called on the carpet.** The boss is **cracking down.**

Mark: I heard. I'll try to **smooth things over.**

Vocabulary

song and dance	n.) excuses
stand on one's own two feet	v.) be independent
give it one's best shot	v.) try very hard
shoot full of holes	v.) find great fault with
up to par (neg.)	adv. or adj.) meeting normal standards
throw cold water on	v.) discourage
call on the carpet	v.) reprimand
crack down	v.) become more strict
smooth something over	v.) make better or more pleasant

Exercise I. *Complete the sentences with the correct idiom.*

a) give it my best shot   b) stand on your own two feet   c) a song and dance   d) throwing cold water on   e) shot it full of holes   f) up to par   g) called him on the carpet   h) smooth things over   i) crack down

1. I want you to clean your room and then do your homework. I don't want to hear _____.
2. I have a headache and don't feel _____.
3. I've never done that work before, but give it to me and I'll _____.
4. She wants to move into her own apartment but her parents are _____ the idea.
5. He is a very poor worker and he's absent a lot. Yesterday the boss _____.
6. They had a big fight but they're trying to _____.
7. You can't be dependent on your family your whole life. You must _____.
8. As soon as he presented his project, the boss showed his displeasure and _____.
9. The police are under pressure to _____ on crime in that neighborhood.

Exercise II. *Rewrite the phrases in italics, using the proper idiomatic expression.*
1. My test scores *have been lower than usual* lately.
2. He's 21 years old and should start *being more independent.*
3. When the family gets together they start arguing. I have to *make the situation more pleasant.*
4. When the mother asked why the child didn't do his chores, he *gave her a lot of excuses.*
5. In order not to be *reprimanded by the boss,* you have to work hard.
6. I want to learn Latin. Please don't *discourage* this idea.
7. He *finds fault with any new ideas I have.*
8. No matter what I do, I *try my best.*
9. The children weren't doing their homework, so we decided to *be stricter.*

Lesson 43. The Apple of One's Eye

Dialogue

Kathy: **Get a load of** that **kid.** She's always **in hot water.**

Jeff: She's **a handful.** I think she's **spoiled.** She is the **apple of her father's eye.**

Kathy: You **hit the nail on the head!** Her family **gets a kick out of** her.

Jeff: She keeps them **in stitches,** but they **give in** too much.

Vocabulary

get a load of	v.) have a good look at
kid	n.) young person
in hot water	adj.) in trouble
a handful	n.) a lot of trouble
spoiled	adj.) getting and expecting everything one wants
apple of one's eye	n.) someone special, usually a son or daughter
hit the nail on the head	v.) arrive at the correct answer, make a precise analysis
get a kick out of	v.) enjoy
in stitches	adj.) laughing
give in	v.) do as others want, surrender

Exercise I. *Complete the sentences with the correct idiom.*

a) kids   b) in hot water   c) in stitches   d) give in   e) spoiled   f) a handful   g) hit the nail on the head
h) apple of his eye   i) get a kick out of   j) get a load of

1. Some people don't like to fight, so they always _____.
2. She's so funny. I'm always _____.
3. You think I'm 32! You're right. You _____.
4. It's a beautiful house. Once you _____ it, you'll love it.
5. That child is terrible. She gets everything she wants. She's _____.
6. Her father thinks she's terrific. She's the _____.
7. I lost my paycheck. I'm _____.
8. That classroom is so noisy. How many _____ are in there?
9. That child is a lot of trouble. She's _____.
10. That child is so intelligent. I enjoy listening to him. I _____ him.

Exercise II. *Rewrite the phrases in italics, using the proper idiomatic expression.*

1. That child *gets too much.*
2. She's *in trouble.*
3. When he tells a joke, I'm always *laughing.*
4. She has four children, but her youngest is *someone special.*
5. I know you don't want to go to the movies, but please *do what I want* for a change.
6. I *enjoy* children who are cute.
7. I don't want to take all those children to the park. They are *a lot of trouble.*
8. That's the date I was born. You *guessed correctly.*
9. That *child* has a lot of energy.
10. *Take a good look at* that Rolls Royce.

Lesson 44. Keeping in Touch

Dialogue

Linda: I've been trying to **track down** some old friends.

Nancy: Haven't you **kept in touch with** them?

Linda: No. We **lost track of** each other.

Nancy: Didn't you ever **come across** any of them?

Linda: A few. Some have **settled down,** some are **tied down,** some are **living it up** and others are **in a rut.**

Nancy: I hope one day you'll all be able to **chew the fat** together.

Vocabulary

track down	v.) search for
keep in touch	v.) communicate, talk or write to each other
lose track of someone	v.) lose contact, not know where someone is
come across	v.) find or meet by chance
settle down	v.) live a quiet, normal life
tied down	adj.) restricted by family or job responsibilities
live it up	v.) pursue pleasure, have a good time
in a rut	adj.) always doing the same thing
chew the fat	v.) chat, talk idly

Exercise I. *Complete the sentences with the correct idiom.*

a) track down   b) live it up   c) settled down   d) chew the fat   e) tied down   f) come across   g) kept in touch   h) in a rut   i) lost track of them

1. I like to meet old friends and _____.
2. My life is always the same. It never changes. I'm _____.
3. When you have children and dogs and a house, you are _____.
4. It's fun to take a vacation and _____.
5. He was a bachelor for many years, but he found the right girl and _____.
6. When looking at old photographs, you _____ a lot of memories.
7. Whatever happened to my former schoolmates? I _____.
8. She was adopted. Now she wants to _____ her biological parents.
9. I telephoned my former high school friend today. I'm glad we _____.

Exercise II. *Rewrite the phrases in italics, using the proper idiomatic expression.*

1. She has three children, a sick mother and a job. *It's difficult for her to get away.*
2. She goes to every party. She likes to *have a good time.*
3. Her son is an hour late for dinner. She's calling his friends trying *to find him.*
4. He moved out of the country and she *had no contact with him.*
5. When he was younger, he was very wild. Now *he leads a very quiet life.*
6. We *had a friendly talk* this afternoon.
7. I was so surprised. I *met him by accident* in the supermarket.
8. Kimiko moved back to Japan but she and Barbara *write to each other.*
9. She never gets out and meets new people. *Her life is always the same.*

Lesson 45.   Hitting It Off

Dialogue
Rachel: I like your friend. She's **down-to-earth.**
Wendy: I know. She's **swell.** We really **hit it off.**
Rachel: I don't like her other friend. She really **turns me off.**
Wendy: I'm surprised they're so **buddy-buddy.**
Rachel: I saw her the other day and she **gave me the cold shoulder.**
Wendy: You're **putting me on!**
Rachel: No—that's about the **size of it.**

Vocabulary

down-to-earth	adj.) having good sense, practical, unpretentious
swell	adj.) terrific
hit it off	v.) enjoy one another's company, get along
turn one off	v.) disgust, bore, repel
buddy-buddy	adj.) very friendly
give (get) the cold shoulder	v.) be unfriendly to, ignore
put someone on	v.) tease, pretend, exaggerate
the size of it	n.) the way it is

Exercise I. *Complete the sentences with the correct idiom.*
a) gave me the cold shoulder   b) turned her off   c) swell   d) putting me on   e) hit it off   f) the size of it   g) down-to-earth   h) buddy-buddy

1. She's friendly and sensible. She's _____.
2. They have been very good friends for years and always go places together. They are _____.
3. She didn't like her sister's new boyfriend at all. He _____.
4. Debbie and Mike enjoy each other's company. I'm glad they _____.
5. We were at a convention and he ignored me. He _____.
6. You got a raise? That's _____.
7. I don't believe you got tickets for a cruise. You're _____.
8. There's nothing you can do. He doesn't want to go to college. That's about _____.

Exercise II. *Rewrite the phrases in italics, using the proper idiomatic expression.*
1. That's a *terrific* idea.
2. They are very rich but *not fancy or pretentious*.
3. They're *very friendly*.
4. I can't eat that food. It *repels me*.
5. That's *the way it is*.
6. I don't believe you got all A's. Don't *exaggerate*.
7. At the party, he *was very unfriendly towards me*.
8. The first time they met, they *got along very well*.

Lesson 46. A Chip Off the Old Block

Dialogue

Mike: Your kid's the **spitting image** of you.
Barbara: He's **a chip off the old block**. He **takes after** my side of the family. He's **nobody's fool.**
Mike: Whom did you **name him after?**
Barbara: A relative who's very **well-off.**
Mike: Do you still see him?
Barbara: **Off and on.** We **steer clear of him** now because he **looks down his nose at** us.

Vocabulary

spitting image	n.) exact resemblance
chip off the old block	n.) child who looks or acts like his or her parent
take after	v.) resemble or act like a parent or relative
nobody's fool	n.) smart, competent person
name someone after	v.) give a child the name of an admired person
well-off	adj.) rich, wealthy
off and on	adv.) occasionally
steer clear of someone	v.) avoid
look down one's nose at	v.) think someone is worthless or unimportant, show contempt

Exercise I. *Complete the sentences with the correct idiom.*

a) chip off the old block   b) spitting image   c) off and on   d) steer clear of   e) looks down her nose at   f) nobody's fool   g) named after   h) takes after   i) well-off

1. When you see trouble, _____ it.
2. They have four new cars, a yacht, a plane and a mansion. They're _____.
3. Her father's name is Robert. Her name is Roberta. She was _____ her father.
4. Her mother is a wonderful cook and so is she. She _____ her mother.
5. She thinks she is better than anyone else. She _____ everyone.
6. He's very smart. He's _____.
7. I watch television _____—it's not a habit.
8. The father was an athlete and his son loves football, baseball and swimming. He's a _____.
9. I knew that was your father. You look exactly alike. You're the _____ of him.

Exercise II. *Rewrite the phrases in italics, using the proper idiomatic expression.*

1. Her father is an excellent artist and she *acts just like* him.
2. Her father died last year. He was a wonderful man and she *gave her son his name.*
3. They don't worry about money. They're *wealthy.*
4. I *occasionally go to the movies.*
5. They ask too many personal questions. Try to *avoid* them.
6. They *show contempt for* anyone who doesn't have as much money as they.
7. Don't worry about him. *He knows what he's doing.*
8. Her mother has a great sense of humor. *So does she.*
9. Are you sure you're not related? *You resemble him exactly.*

Lesson 47. Seeing Eye to Eye

Dialogue
Dan: He doesn't **have a mind of his own.**

Joe: That's true. His wife **leads him around by the nose.**

Dan: Why doesn't he **give her a piece of his mind?** I'd **put my foot down.**

Joe: She's always **at odds** with him. They never **see eye to eye.**

Dan: I know she always **puts him down.**

Joe: He should **stick up for** himself.

Vocabulary

have a mind of one's own	v.) be able to think independently
lead one around by the nose	v.) have full control of, make someone do what you want
give someone a piece of one's mind	v.) say what you really think when angry
put one's foot down	v.) object strongly, take firm preventive action
at odds	adj.) in disagreement
see eye to eye	v.) have the same opinion, agree
put down	v.) make someone look bad, criticize
stick up for	v.) defend, help, support

Exercise I. *Complete the sentences with the correct idiom.*
a) puts her down   b) a piece of her mind   c) see eye to eye   d) have a mind of her own   e) at odds
f) put your foot down   g) sticks up for   h) leads him around by the nose

1. Don't talk about his family. He _____ them.
2. That wife tells her husband what to do all the time. She _____.
3. My friend and I think alike. We _____.
4. If you don't want to work overtime every night, _____.
5. She was so angry, she gave him _____.
6. They don't get along well. They're always _____ with each other.
7. He always calls her "stupid." I don't like the way he _____.
8. She always agrees with her husband. She doesn't _____.

Exercise II. *Rewrite the phrases in italics, using the proper idiomatic expression.*
1. John always *defends* his friends.
2. She always *criticizes* her child.
3. They usually *agree* on how to raise their child.
4. They got a divorce because they were always *disagreeing* with each other.
5. I would *object strongly* if my child wanted to smoke.
6. When my friend didn't come to my dinner party, I *told her how angry I was.*
7. She *makes him do whatever she wants.*
8. Never mind what your father says, *can't you think for yourself?*

Lesson 48.   On the Rocks

Dialogue

Hillary: Is it a **false alarm** or is their marriage really **on the rocks?**
Sandy: Well, the marriage has been **on shaky ground** but they haven't **split up** yet.
Hillary: I wonder who's **at fault?**
Sandy: I don't know but I don't think they're **on the same wavelength.**
Hillary: If I know her, she's **making the best of it.** I hope she **works things out.**

Vocabulary

false alarm	n.) warning or report that's untrue
on the rocks	adj.) breaking up, ruined
on shaky ground	adj.) unstable
split up	v.) separate
at fault	adj.) responsible, to blame
on the same wavelength	adj.) communicating, thinking similarly
make the best of	v.) accept a bad situation and do as well as possible under the circumstances
work out	v.) find an answer, solve

Exercise I. *Complete the sentences with the correct idiom.*

a) making the best of   b) at fault   c) on the same wavelength   d) false alarm   e) shaky ground
f) split up   g) on the rocks   h) work it out

1. The police thought there was a robbery at the bank but it was a _____.
2. He broke his leg and can't move very well, but he's cheerful and _____ it.
3. They're getting a divorce. I didn't know their marriage was _____.
4. This math problem is hard, but I'm trying to _____.
5. That new government is on _____.
6. They were a very nice couple. I was sorry to hear they _____.
7. All the milk is on the floor. Who's _____?
8. They didn't understand each other. They weren't _____.

Exercise II. *Rewrite the phrases in italics, using the proper idiomatic expression.*

1. Their marriage is *breaking up*.
2. If it rains everyday while you're on vacation, you have to *accept it and do the best you can*.
3. I don't want you to be unhappy. We'll *find an answer to this problem*.
4. They *don't think alike*.
5. That's *an untrue report*.
6. That business is *unstable*.
7. Who's *responsible* for breaking that window?
8. After ten years of marriage, they decided to get a divorce. They *separated* last week.

Lesson 49. An Old Flame

Dialogue

Eddie: Was that your **old flame?**

Harry: Yeah—we met on a **blind date.**

Eddie: Did you **fall for** her?

Harry: **Like a ton of bricks.** I stopped **playing the field** and asked her to **go steady.**

Eddie: Did you ever **pop the question?**

Harry: Sure, but at first she couldn't **make up her mind.** Then she **turned me down.**

Vocabulary

old flame	n.) former girlfriend or boyfriend
blind date	n.) date arranged for two people who don't know each other
fall for	v.) begin to love, have strong emotions for
like a ton of bricks	adv.) strongly, forcefully
play the field	v.) go out with many people romantically
go steady	v.) go out with only one person romantically
pop the question	v.) ask to marry
make up one's mind	v.) decide
turn someone down	v.) reject

Exercise I. *Complete the sentences with the correct idiom.*

a) make up your mind   b) hit him like a ton of bricks   c) playing the field   d) going steady   e) old flame   f) pop the question   g) blind date   h) fell for   i) turned me down

1. I didn't know you were getting married. When did he _____?
2. Where did you want to go—to the movies or bowling? It's getting late. _____.
3. I wasn't qualified for that job so they _____.
4. Tom and Ann are not going out with anyone else. They've been _____ for a year.
5. They didn't know each other before. A friend arranged their _____.
6. He was in love with her many years ago. She's an _____.
7. He thought she was so beautiful. He _____ her.
8. He doesn't want to get married. He enjoys _____.
9. He didn't know his favorite uncle died. The news of his death _____.

Exercise II. *Rewrite the phrases in italics, using the proper idiomatic expression.*

1. *We're going out tonight but I never met him before.*
2. She wanted to join that club but they *rejected her.*
3. That's his *old girlfriend.*
4. Please *decide* what you want for dinner.
5. After going out with her several times, he *started to love* her.
6. When did he *ask you to marry him?*
7. She didn't cry when she heard about his death, but later *she felt it very strongly.*
8. They are *seeing each other exclusively.*
9. He's too young to get married. He wants to *go out with many girls.*

Lesson 50. A Wet Blanket

Dialogue

Beth: I know John's a **wet blanket** and **puts a damper on** everything. He has no **get up and go.**

Peter: **Fix him up** with Mary. She's **a live wire.** I used to **have a crush on** her myself, but she **dumped** me.

Beth: What if she **stands John up?**

Peter: He'll **yell bloody murder.**

Vocabulary

wet blanket	n.) person who discourages others from having fun
put a damper on	v.) discourage, spoil a person's fun
get up and go	n.) ambition, energy, enthusiasm
fix someone up	v.) arrange a date for
live wire	n.) active, exciting person
have a crush on	v.) be attracted to
dump	v.) get rid of, reject
stand someone up	v.) fail to keep an appointment or date
yell (scream) bloody murder	v.) express loud, emotional anger

Exercise I. *Complete the sentences with the correct idiom.*

a) fix her friends up   b) put a damper on   c) wet blanket   d) get up and go   e) dumped him   f) live wire   g) yell bloody murder   h) have crushes on   i) stood you up

1. Ann was no fun at that party. She was a _____.
2. He always hired people who had _____.
3. I was very happy today until my boss came to work in a bad mood. That _____ everything.
4. She's very romantic. She likes to _____ with one another.
5. People want her at their parties because she's a _____.
6. Some babies will _____ if their mothers leave them with babysitters.
7. Many teenagers _____ movie stars.
8. My car broke down and I couldn't keep my appointment. I'm sorry I _____.
9. She doesn't go out with him anymore. She met someone new, so she _____.

Exercise II. *Rewrite the phrases in italics, using the proper idiomatic expression.*

1. He always *has loud, emotional bursts of anger.*
2. I was very surprised that he *rejected* her.
3. She is a *very exciting person to have around.*
4. He has a lot of *ambition.*
5. *He discourages everyone from having fun.*
6. *He didn't show up for our meeting.*
7. I didn't know she *was attracted to* that football player.
8. If you like him, I'll *get you a date* with him.
9. I want to go into business so please don't *discourage me.*

Lesson 51. A Knockout

Dialogue

Stacy: I know she's a **knockout** and he's **nuts about** her but he's **playing with fire.**

Wendy: She **twists him around her little finger** and **leads him on.** He's **at her beck and call.**

Stacy: Why does he **put her on a pedestal?**

Wendy: Because she **plays up to him** and **pours it on thick.**

Vocabulary

a knockout	n.) a beautiful person or thing
nuts about	adj.) in love with, enthusiastic about
play with fire	v.) invite danger, trouble
twist someone around one's finger	v.) influence someone easily
lead on	v.) insincerely encourage
at one's beck and call	adj.) always ready to do as ordered
put someone on a pedestal	v.) idolize, worship
play up to someone	v.) flatter or please for selfish reasons
pour (spread, put, lay) it on thick	v.) flatter profusely, exaggerate

Exercise I. *Complete the sentences with the correct idiom.*

a) lay it on thick   b) twist him around her little finger   c) leading him on   d) playing with fire
e) puts her on a pedestal   f) at his beck and call   g) nuts about   h) a knockout   i) playing up to him

1. He wanted to go home early so he said he had a headache. Nobody really believed him so he had to _____.
2. Did you notice that beautiful girl? She was _____.
3. If you experiment with drugs, you're _____.
4. Chocolate ice cream is her favorite food. She is _____ it.
5. She can make him do whatever she wants. It's amazing how she can _____.
6. He is in love with her but she is not in love with him. Why does she make him believe she loves him by _____?
7. I don't understand why he idolizes her. He _____.
8. He can call her at any time of night and she will come running. She is _____.
9. She is going to make sure she gets the job by _____.

Exercise II. *Rewrite the phrases in italics, using the proper idiomatic expression.*

1. *She will do whatever he says.*
2. He *worships her.*
3. He is *very enthusiastic about* golf.
4. She *has a lot of influence over him.*
5. She is *looking for trouble.*
6. He goes out with a lot of girls but he is *trying to make her* believe she is the only one.
7. She is a *terrific looking girl.*
8. He wanted a raise, so he tried to *be especially nice to* his boss.
9. Although her dress was ugly, he told her it was the prettiest one he's seen. *That is some exaggeration.*

Lesson 52.   A Sourpuss

Dialogue

Lynn: She's a **sourpuss.** How does he **put up with** her?
Ruth: I think she **wears the pants** in the family. She **keeps tabs on** everything.
Lynn: If he steps **out of line,** she'll **fix his wagon.** She **pushes him around.**
Ruth: He has to **weigh his words** when he talks to her.
Lynn: You can see she **rules the roost.**

Vocabulary

sourpuss	n.) a disagreeable person who seldom smiles
put up with	v.) patiently accept, endure
wear the pants	v.) be the boss of a family
keep tabs on	v.) watch, check
out of line	adj.) not usual, incorrect, unacceptable
fix one's wagon	v.) make trouble for someone, retaliate
push someone around	v.) boss, make a person do what you want
weigh one's words	v.) be careful of what one says
rule the roost	v.) be the dominant one in the family

Exercise I. *Complete the sentences with the correct idiom.*

a) out of line   b) wears the pants   c) keep tabs on   d) sourpuss   e) put up with   f) pushed me around
g) weigh my words   h) fix his wagon   i) rules the roost

1. She tells everybody in the family what to do. She _____.
2. I don't like to be around him. He never smiles. He is a _____.
3. His mother said he better be home for dinner but he's late again. She's going to _____.
4. The boss is going to interview me today. I don't think I should talk too much. I better _____.
5. Her son has been getting into trouble lately, so she's had to _____ him.
6. She tells her husband exactly what he can and cannot do. She _____.
7. Her children bring home friends all hours of the night. I wouldn't _____ it.
8. The principal is coming to our classroom this afternoon. I want excellent behavior. You will be punished if you get _____.
9. I always had to listen to my older sister. She _____.

Exercise II. *Rewrite the phrases in italics, using the proper idiomatic expression.*

1. You have to *be careful what you say* in front of him.
2. His behavior is *not acceptable.*
3. She *is the boss of the family.*
4. He is a *very unpleasant person who doesn't smile.*
5. I don't understand how she *patiently endures* his bad temper.
6. She didn't like what he did, and she's going to *retaliate.*
7. He has been getting into a lot of trouble lately. You better *watch* him.
8. In that household, *everyone listens to what she says.*
9. Don't let him *make you do what he wants.*

Lesson 53.   A Lemon

Dialogue

George: It's too bad he bought a **lemon.**
Barbara: Yeah, but I think he's **handy.** I'm **all thumbs.**
George: Anything I get **falls apart.** Then I have to **cough up** money to get it fixed.
Barbara: I'm **having a fit.** I have to **scrape together** some **dough.** My TV is **on the blink.**

Vocabulary

lemon	n.) merchandise that doesn't work
handy	adj.) can fix things; useful
all thumbs	adj.) can't fix things; clumsy
fall apart	v.) deteriorate; stop working properly
cough up	v.) give money unwillingly; give up a secret
have a fit	v.) become upset
scrape together	v.) get money little by little
dough	n.) money
on the blink	adj.) not working

Exercise I. *Complete the sentences with the correct idiom.*

a) have a fit   b) cough up   c) lemon   d) all thumbs   e) handy   f) scrape together   g) on the blink
h) fall apart   i) dough

1. My TV doesn't work. It's _____.
2. If my child comes home late, I _____.
3. That brand-new car doesn't run well. It's a _____.
4. He can fix anything. He's very _____.
5. She can't sew, knit or crochet. She's _____.
6. Christmas is coming. I have to _____ some money.
7. I don't like to buy children's toys because they always _____.
8. I wish I made a lot of _____.
9. He doesn't want to get married, but she's making him _____ money for a diamond ring.

Exercise II. *Rewrite the phrases in italics, using the proper idiomatic expression.*

1. The phone *isn't working.*
2. Let him assemble the bookcase. *He can fix anything.*
3. That car *never worked well.*
4. Your toy broke? I can't fix it. I'm *too clumsy.*
5. His calculator always *breaks down.*
6. I hate to pay my electric bill, but eventually *I send the money.*
7. I spent all my *money.*
8. I *become upset* when people are late.
9. I'm having trouble *getting money* to buy a new car.

Lesson 54.   High and Low

Dialogue

Mike: I've looked **high and low** for my wallet.
Debbie: I see. This place is a **mess.**
Mike: I'll **straighten it out.**
Debbie: You **pile everything up** and **scatter things around.** You're a **slob.**
Mike: It'll **turn up.** It's probably **right under my nose.**
Debbie: Here it is, finally. I'm tired. Let's **hit the sack.**

Vocabulary

high and low	adv.) every place
mess	n.) disorderly, cluttered condition; bad or confused situation
straighten out (up)	v.) put in order
pile up	v.) accumulate; put things on top of each other
scatter around	v.) carelessly put in different places
slob	n.) person who isn't clean and neat
turn up	v.) appear
right under one's nose	adv.) in an obvious, nearby place
hit the sack	v.) go to bed

Exercise I. *Complete the sentences with the correct idiom.*

a) scattered around   b) turn up   c) mess   d) pile up   e) high and low   f) slob   g) hit the sack
h) straighten them out   i) right under my nose

1. I can't find my glasses. They'll _____ when I don't need them.
2. I want to go to sleep. Let's _____.
3. Your room hasn't been cleaned and it's a _____.
4. Your books and toys are all over the floor. Please _____.
5. He always spills wine on his suit. He is a _____.
6. I looked all over for my keys. They were on the table. They were _____.
7. My sister lives in Illinois. My parents live in Florida. We're _____.
8. _____ a lot of meat and salad on that sandwich. I'm hungry.
9. I can't find my glasses anywhere. I've looked _____.

Exercise II. *Rewrite the phrases in italics, using the proper idiomatic expression.*

1. Her son keeps *putting his toys in different places.*
2. Let's *go to sleep.*
3. He didn't forget the appointment. He'll *appear.*
4. *Put your desk in order.*
5. I've looked *every place* for that book.
6. He can't pay the money he owes, his job is awful, and his wife is getting a divorce. His life is a real *bad situation.*
7. I have so much work. It just keeps *increasing.*
8. He's *not a neat person.*
9. Don't worry. My keys were practically *in front of me.*

Lesson 55.   The Boob Tube

Dialogue

Jessica: Your **boob tube** is on **its last legs.** The picture is going **haywire.**

Andrew: It's been **on the fritz** lately. I hope it doesn't **bite the dust** before payday.

Jessica: Let me **fiddle around** with it. Maybe I can **doctor it up.**

Andrew: Uh oh, I can **kiss that goodbye.**

Vocabulary

boob tube	n.) television set
on one's last legs	adj.) at the end of one's strength or usefulness
haywire	adj.) broken, confused, awry
on the fritz	adj.) not working correctly, out of order
bite the dust	v.) die, disappear
fiddle around	v.) work without a definite plan or knowledge
doctor up	v.) fix superficially or temporarily
kiss something goodbye	v.) see something ruined or lost

Exercise I. *Complete the sentences with the correct idiom.*

a) fiddle around   b) bit the dust   c) on its last legs   d) on the fritz   e) haywire   f) doctor it up   g) boob tube   h) kiss it goodbye

1. My car is giving me a lot of trouble. I don't think it can be fixed. It's _____.
2. My meal is ruined. What can I do to _____?
3. Tonight is going to be very boring. Nothing is on the _____.
4. My child's toy doesn't work. I think I'll _____ with it.
5. Nobody cared about my idea to increase business. I guess that idea _____.
6. We had many plans for our vacation but it rained and everything went _____.
7. He doesn't know what he's doing. If he tries to fix it, you can _____.
8. My car didn't start this morning. The battery is _____.

Exercise II. *Rewrite the phrases in italics, using the proper idiomatic expression.*

1. My muffler is hanging from my car. I am going to have to *temporarily fix it.*
2. He was going to become a teacher but when he found out what they earned, *he gave up that idea.*
3. After the death of his father, his whole life *became confused.*
4. I think I'll go home and watch *television.*
5. I worked eight hours, went home and made dinner, cleaned up the house, did some laundry and helped the children with their homework. *I have no more strength.*
6. I don't get a clear picture on my television. *It isn't working right.*
7. *He's trying to work that computer but he doesn't know exactly what he is doing.*
8. He doesn't know how to work that camera. *That film is going to be ruined.*

Lesson 56.   Sprucing Up

Dialogue
John: We'll have to start **from scratch** to **spruce up** this house. It's really **going to pot.**
Sue: Maybe we could **scrounge around** for some **second-hand** furniture and other **stuff.**
John: I would like to make the house larger. We could use some mcre **elbow room.** I'm beginning
        to feel **hemmed in.**
Sue: Forget it. Where are we going to **dig up** the **loot** for major repairs?

Vocabulary
from scratch   adv.) from the very beginning; starting with raw materials
spruce up   v.) clean, redecorate
go to pot   v.) deteriorate; become undisciplined, unkempt
scrounge around   v.) look in a lot of places for a certain item
second-hand   adj.) not new, previously used
stuff   n.) things
elbow room   n.) enough space to be comfortable
hemmed in   adj.) crowded, cramped, uncomfortable
dig up   v.) find, recall, discover
loot   n.) money

Exercise I. *Complete the sentences with the correct idiom.*
a) scrounge around   b) from scratch   c) sprucing up   d) went to pot   e) stuff   f) loot   g) elbow room
h) second-hand   i) hemmed in   j) dig up

1. The best apple pie is one made _____.
2. I have no money. I'll have to _____ and see if there's any money in the house.
3. That's a fancy car. How much _____ will I need to buy it?
4. When springtime comes, most people feel like _____ clothes.
5. Sometimes it's better not to _____ memories of the past.
6. Usually the second or third child in a family gets _____ clothes.
7. When I play golf, I don't want people all around me. I need _____.
8. It's amazing how much _____ you can fit into your closet.
9. When there are too many people in one room, I feel _____.
10. That house used to be very well kept. Now it's in very bad condition. It _____.

Exercise II. *Rewrite the phrases in italics, using the proper idiomatic expression.*
1. It's too crowded. I need more *space.*
2. I'm *looking for* some junk food in this house.
3. That's a lot of *money.*
4. You have a lot of beautiful *things.*
5. Let's *redecorate* the house.
6. What did you *find* in the basement?
7. You can't sell *used* merchandise in that store.
8. Let's not use a cake mix. Let's start *from the beginning.*
9. It was a beautiful neighborhood many years ago. It's too bad it *deteriorated.*
10. I like the open spaces of the country. Whenever I'm in the city, I feel *cramped.*

Lesson 57.   A Pad

Dialogue

Ellen: If you want a decent **pad** in that city, you have to pay **under the table.**
Scott: You're led on a **wild goose chase** if you look for an apartment in the papers.
Ellen: The apartment I saw today was so **run-down.**
Scott: Maybe you could improve it if you use a lot of **elbow grease.**
Ellen: Nothing will help. I like everything **spic and span.** When anything is **topsy-turvy,** it **turns my stomach.**

Vocabulary

pad	n.) apartment
under the table	adv.) illegal money transaction, such as paying a bribe
wild goose chase	n.) absurd or hopeless search
run-down	adj.) in bad condition
elbow grease	n.) strength for cleaning
spic and span	adj.) very clean, very neat
topsy-turvy	adj.) upside down, in disarray
turn someone's stomach	v.) get someone sick and upset

Exercise I. *Complete the sentences with the correct idiom.*

a) wild goose chase   b) elbow grease   c) run-down   d) pads   e) spic and span   f) topsy-turvy   g) under the table   h) turns my stomach

1. Most teenagers want to get their own _____.
2. Some people are collecting unemployment insurance even though they have a job where they're paid
   _____.
3. I'm sorry to say that some children mistreat elders. It _____.
4. When you move from one apartment to another, everything is _____.
5. She didn't want the police to know where her boyfriend was, so she gave them false information which led them on a _____.
6. I'm working very hard but not eating or sleeping properly. I think I'm _____.
7. If you want that car to shine, use a little _____.
8. She's always cleaning. Her apartment is _____.

Exercise II. *Rewrite the phrases in italics, using the proper idiomatic expression.*

1. Greasy food *gets me sick.*
2. She's a neat child. Her room is *very clean.*
3. That building is *in bad condition.*
4. The politician took *a bribe.*
5. She has a cute *apartment.*
6. They sent me *from one place to another with no reason.*
7. That floor is so dirty, you'll need a lot of *strength* to clean it.
8. All my clothes are *thrown into my closet.*

Lesson 58.   Hitting the Bottle

Dialogue
Lisa: They were only married for a year before they **broke up.**
Elaine: What was her **beef?**
Lisa: She said he was **hitting the bottle** too much.
Elaine: Do you think they'll **patch things up?**
Lisa: Only if he **turns over a new leaf.**
Elaine: He won't. He's going to **keep on** drinking. He has no **will power.**
Lisa: He can do it if he goes **cold turkey.**

Vocabulary
break up   v.) separate
beef   n.) complaint
hit the bottle   v.) drink alcohol
patch up   v.) fix
turn over a new leaf   v.) change one's conduct for the better
keep on   v.) continue
will power   n.) strength of mind
go cold turkey   v.) stop abruptly

Exercise I. *Complete the sentences with the correct idiom.*
a) your beef b) cold turkey c) patch things up d) hit the bottle e) turns over a new leaf f) will power g) break up h) keep on

1. He gave up smoking. He has more _____ than I do.
2. I don't want to argue. Let's _____.
3. Why are you angry? What's _____?
4. They aren't happy together. They're going to _____.
5. He lost his job because he _____.
6. He just got out of jail. I hope he _____.
7. He stopped smoking right away. He went _____.
8. If you're not hungry, don't _____ eating.

Exercise II. *Rewrite the phrases in italics, using the proper idiomatic expression.*
1. What's your *complaint?*
2. Let's *fix everything.*
3. Don't smoke another cigarette. *Stop now.*
4. He's *drinking liquor* again.
5. If I want to quit smoking, I can. I have the *strength.*
6. They *aren't seeing each other any more.*
7. *He's never going to lie or steal again.*
8. It's not 5 P.M.—*continue* working.

Lesson 59. In the Same Boat

Dialogue
David: He's a **nag**. He keeps **hounding** me.
Eugene: I'm **in the same boat**. He won't **get off my back**. He has a **one-track mind**.
David: Well, you **call the shots**. You have to **draw the line** somewhere.
Eugene: Maybe I should tell him to **knock it off**.
David: I just wish he'd **take a powder**.

Vocabulary
a nag   n.) a persistently urging person
hound   v.) continually bother, go after
in the same boat   adv. or adj.) in a similar situation
get off one's back   v.) leave someone alone, don't bother
one-track mind   n.) mind focused on a single idea
call the shots   v.) be in charge, give orders
draw the line   v.) set a limit
knock it off   v.) stop
take a powder   v.) leave quickly, run away

Exercise I. *Complete the sentences with the correct idiom.*
a) calls the shots   b) get him off her back   c) nag   d) draw the line   e) hound   f) took a powder
g) in the same boat   h) knock it off   i) one-track mind

1. When the police arrived, the burglars _____.
2. She's always telling me to take out the garbage. She's a _____.
3. My boss's car broke down. My train stalled. We both got to work late. We were _____.
4. Mothers usually _____ their children to study and brush their teeth.
5. The child constantly kept asking for candy and the mother finally gave him some to

   _____.
6. You can't have it. Don't ask anymore. _____.
7. I don't mind if he goes out on the weekend but he's got schoolwork and I _____ on weekdays.
8. When his parents are away, his older brother _____.
9. All he ever thinks about is football. He has a _____.

Exercise II. *Rewrite the phrases in italics, using the proper idiomatic expression.*
1. *Stop it.*
2. *Go away.*
3. I told you "no." Stop *asking me all the time.*
4. I understand your problem because *I have the same one.*
5. His father died and now *he's in control of the company.*
6. You cannot have a new car. *Don't bother me anymore.*
7. He is only interested in cars. *He thinks about nothing else.*
8. They have to know when to come home. You must *set a limit.*
9. She is *the kind of person who urges you to do something over and over again.*

Lesson 60.   A Pill

Dialogue
Tammy: He's a **pill.** He keeps **harping on** the same thing.
Holly: He also **nitpicks.** It **drives me up a wall.**
Tammy: It doesn't **sit right** with me either. I don't like **splitting hairs.**
Holly: I shouldn't **take it to heart,** but he's going to send me to the **looney bin.**

Vocabulary
pill	n.) an annoying, disagreeable person
harp on	v.) dwell on one subject, repeat, persist
nitpick	v.) look for very minor errors or problems
drive someone up a wall	v.) make someone crazy
sit right (neg.)	v.) be acceptable
split hairs	v.) make trivial, unnecessary distinctions
take something to heart	v.) consider seriously
looney bin	n.) insane asylum

Exercise I. *Complete the sentences with the correct idiom.*
a) taken it to heart   b) split hairs   c) drive me up a wall   d) pill   e) harping on   f) nitpick   g) looney bin   h) sit right

1. If he doesn't stop singing that song over and over again, he will _____.
2. Whenever you see her, she is never feeling well and always complaining. She is a _____.
3. I know I made a mistake but stop _____ it.
4. Somebody better talk to him about the way he eats. His table manners don't _____ with our family.
5. Whenever you submit a report to him, he will look for any minor, unimportant errors. He loves to _____.
6. These children can make you crazy. Living with them is like living in a _____.
7. His parents had a talk with him about improving his grades. I hope he has _____.
8. It's important that we all work together on this project. If we want the project done quickly we cannot _____.

Exercise II. *Rewrite the phrases in italics, using the proper idiomatic expression.*
1. I would like you to *seriously consider* what I said.
2. This place is like *an insane asylum.*
3. Don't *worry about differences that are unimportant.*
4. These teenagers are going to *make me crazy.*
5. She's a *very annoying person.*
6. Consider the whole idea and stop *looking for unimportant minor details.*
7. *I don't think his behavior is acceptable.*
8. She keeps *telling everyone over and over* her ideas about business.

Lesson 61.   Dishing It Out

Dialogue
Debbie: I have a **bone to pick with you.**
Mike: Okay. Let's **clear the air.** What are you **getting at?**
Debbie: You always have **a chip on your shoulder.**
Mike: I'm sorry. I don't mean to **get your goat.**
Debbie: It seems you can **dish it out** but you can't **take it.**
Mike: Don't worry. In the future, I'll start **whistling a different tune.**

Vocabulary
bone to pick with someone	n.) complaint, dispute, argument
clear the air	v.) calm anger and remove misunderstanding
get at	v.) mean, hint
chip on one's shoulder	n.) quarrelsome attitude, quick to anger
get one's goat	v.) make someone disgusted, annoyed, angry
dish out	v.) criticize, abuse, scold
take it	v.) endure trouble, criticism, abuse, pressure
whistle a different tune	v.) change one's attitude, contradict previous ideas

Exercise I. *Complete the sentences with the correct idiom.*
a) a bone to pick with her   b) whistles a different tune   c) cleared the air   d) dish it out   e) chip on his shoulder   f) take it   g) getting at   h) got his goat

1. The boss's son doesn't believe his father should pay overtime, but when he can work extra hours, he _____.
2. When Bill and Bob were angry, Bob made a joke and it _____ between them.
3. You're hinting at something. What are you _____?
4. Sometimes he's nasty and insulting. He can _____.
5. He gets very upset when someone criticizes him. He can't _____.
6. His secretary takes four coffee breaks. He has _____.
7. The slow service in the restaurant _____.
8. He angers easily. Be careful what you say to him. He has a _____.

Exercise II. *Rewrite the phrases in italics, using the proper idiomatic expression.*
1. *He's always looking for an argument.*
2. Before he was a father, he said he would never punish his child. Now that he has two children, he *has changed his whole attitude.*
3. His television was fixed poorly. He called them and said he had a *complaint.*
4. *What do you mean?*
5. Every day he parks in my parking place. *He gets me very angry.*
6. I couldn't stand all that pressure, but she can *handle it.*
7. Nobody likes to be around her because she *is so critical.*
8. *I don't want bad feelings between us.*

Lesson 62. Settling the Score

Dialogue
Ray: He **made a monkey out of me** with his **wisecracks** about my abilities.
Sid: Don't **flip your lid. Let bygones be bygones.**
Ray: **Not on your life.** I'm going to **settle the score.**
Sid: You should have a **man-to-man** talk and **have it out** instead of trying to **get even.**

Vocabulary
make a monkey out of someone	v.) cause to look foolish
wisecrack	n.) sarcastic or nasty remark
flip one's lid	v.) get angry; go crazy; become very excited
Let bygones be bygones.	Forget differences that happened in the past.
Not on your life.	Definitely not, no way.
settle the score	v.) retaliate, pay someone back for a past hurt
man-to-man	adj.) frank, direct
have it out with someone	v.) discuss a conflict or misunderstanding with the other person involved
get even	v.) get revenge, settle the score

Exercise I. *Complete the sentences with the correct idiom.*
a) made a monkey out of   b) wisecracks   c) let bygones be bygones   d) get even   e) had it out with
f) man-to-man   g) not on your life   h) settle the score   i) flip her lid

1. You haven't spoken to your sister in years. Now that she's sick, why don't you _____?
2. He's not very pleasant, so don't be upset if he makes _____ about your clothes.
3. The lawyer was very shrewd and _____ the opponent's client.
4. She wants to get married, but I don't want to. I told her, "_____."
5. Her boyfriend married someone else. She was very upset and she wants to _____.
6. Don't discuss this problem with me. Go directly to the boss's office and have a _____ talk with him.
7. When my wife hears I lost my job, she's going to _____.
8. He doesn't realize that he hurt you. It would be a good idea if you met and _____ him.
9. When I was a child, that man cheated my family. Now that I am older, I am going to _____.

Exercise II. *Rewrite the phrases in italics, using the proper idiomatic expression.*
1. Have a *frank* talk with him.
2. It's not a good idea to *get revenge.*
3. I wouldn't live there. *No way.*
4. He made *nasty jokes* about her family.
5. She *made him look very foolish.*
6. *Forget about past differences.*
7. Some people find it necessary to *pay somebody back* for past hurts.
8. I think you should *discuss this problem* with him.
9. When the boy's father saw the wrecked car, he *got very angry.*

Lesson 63. The Last Straw

Dialogue
Sam: That was **the last straw.** I don't like people **making fun of me.**
Nick: **Just shrug it off. Don't make a mountain out of a molehill.**
Sam: If he does it again, the **fur will fly.**
Nick: Don't **make waves.**
Sam: If I don't **nip it in the bud,** he'll keep doing it.
Nick: If I were you, I'd **bury the hatchet.**

Vocabulary

the last straw	n.) the last insult or injury that one can endure
make fun of	v.) ridicule
shrug off	v.) not be bothered or hurt, dismiss
make a mountain out of a molehill	v.) make a big problem out of a small one
the fur will fly, make the fur fly	v.) create a disturbance
make waves	v.) upset the status quo, create a disturbance
nip in the bud	v.) prevent at the start
bury the hatchet	v.) make peace, stop arguing

Exercise I. *Complete the sentences with the correct idiom.*
a) last straw b) make fun of c) nip it in the bud d) shrugged off e) make waves f) make a mountain out of a molehill g) bury the hatchet h) fur's going to fly

1. They have been fighting for years. I don't think they will ever _____.
2. It wasn't difficult. It was easy. Don't _____.
3. When your child starts smoking, it's best to _____.
4. The baseball pitcher _____ the booing of the fans.
5. He lost all his money at the racetrack. When he gets home, the _____.
6. Some people avoid controversy. They don't like to _____.
7. Her son watched TV all day and didn't work. When he started to gamble, she was furious. That was the _____.
8. It's not nice to _____ people.

Exercise II. *Rewrite the phrases in italics, using the proper idiomatic expression.*
1. You have to *stop bad habits in the beginning.*
2. I do everything in that office. Nobody helps me. When the boss asked me to make coffee, too, that was *the end.*
3. I know you're upset, but *don't let it bother you.*
4. It would be nice to see them *stop arguing.*
5. Everything is going well. Don't *make any problems.*
6. When he sees the teenagers scratch his car with their bicycles, *there's going to be a big argument.*
7. That is such a little problem. Don't *make it bigger than it is.*
8. He was getting very angry because another student was *ridiculing* his friend.

Lesson 64.   A Kick in the Pants

Dialogue
Jean: Why does he always **jump down your throat?**
Gail: I don't know. I try to be **fair and square** but all I get is a **kick in the pants.** I feel like I'm **knocking my head against the wall.**
Jean: It **serves you right** because you allow him to **walk all over you.**
Gail: Don't **rub it in.** I don't like getting **the short end of the stick.**

Vocabulary

jump down someone's throat	v.) criticize angrily, hastily
fair and square	adj. or adv.) honest; honestly
kick in the pants (teeth)	n.) rejection, criticism
knock one's head against the wall	v.) waste time in futile effort to improve or change something
serve someone right	v.) give due punishment
walk all over someone	v.) take advantage of someone
rub something in	v.) constantly refer to a mistake or fault
short end of the stick	n.) unfair, unequal treatment

Exercise I. *Complete the sentences with the correct idiom.*
a) knocking your head against the wall   b) fair and square   c) rubbing it in   d) it serves her right
e) the short end of the stick   f) a kick in the pants   g) walks all over him   h) jumps down my throat

1. This is the third time I have to stay late. Everybody else leaves at 5:00. I'm getting _____.

2. You are trying to make teenagers understand that driving fast is dangerous? You're _____.

3. It's very important for parents to be _____ with their children.
4. The child ate all the chocolate candy and got sick. _____.
5. He's very angry today. Anytime I ask him a question, he _____.
6. He loves her so much and she takes advantage of him. She _____.
7. Joe was very kind to a poor, unfortunate person and when that person made a lot of money, he ignored Joe. Joe got _____.
8. I know it was a stupid thing to do, but you don't have to keep _____.

Exercise II. *Rewrite the phrases in italics, using the proper idiomatic expression.*
1. After a big dinner, everybody watches TV while I clean up the dishes. I *get unfair treatment.*
2. I keep telling her that smoking is harmful to her health, but it is just *wasted effort.*
3. It is always best to be *frank and honest.*
4. He is always *criticizing someone angrily.*
5. Unfortunately, sometimes when you do something nice, you *are met with rejection that is unexpected.*
6. If you go outside in the winter without a coat, you'll get a cold. *It will be due punishment.*
7. It is too bad that some people *take advantage of* others.
8. Her child made a mistake and she keeps *referring to it.*

Lesson 65.   A Bum Ticker

Dialogue

Dottie: If he didn't have a **bum ticker,** I'd **put him in his place.**

Jimmy: **Don't do anything rash.** I think you have to **bite your tongue** when he's **on the warpath.**

Dottie: But he doesn't have to make a **federal case** out of it.

Jimmy: I know he's a **lulu.** He doesn't **give a hoot** whom he **bawls out.**

Vocabulary

bum ticker	n.) weak or diseased heart
put someone in his or her place	v.) scold someone for rude, improper behavior
do something rash	v.) take drastic action
bite one's tongue	v.) keep oneself from speaking
on the warpath	adj.) very angry, looking for trouble
make a federal case out of some-thing	v.) overreact, take strong measures for a minor problem
lulu	n.) a person with unconventional, exaggerated behavior; an eccentric character
give a hoot (neg.)	v.) care
bawl out	v.) reprimand

Exercise I. *Complete the sentences with the correct idiom.*

a) do anything rash   b) bite my tongue   c) federal case   d) on the warpath   e) put her in her place
f) bum ticker   g) give a hoot   h) bawl him out   i) lulu

1. I didn't want to get into an argument, so I had to _____.
2. She's very rude. Someone should _____.
3. When Mary saw John with another girl, she went _____.
4. He's overweight and smokes three packs of cigarettes a day. That's why he has a _____.
5. At one time he loved her very much, but now he doesn't _____ about her.
6. He got a bad grade. His father will _____.
7. I know school is difficult but please don't quit. Think about it before you _____.
8. He'll lie and cheat every chance he gets. He's a _____.
9. I didn't do well on a test and now I can't go out for a month. Why are my parents making a _____ out of it?

Exercise II. *Rewrite the phrases in italics, using the proper idiomatic expression.*

1. If he does anything wrong, his parents *reprimand him.*
2. He has a *bad heart.*
3. If you are angry, *hold back from speaking.*
4. He didn't get an important telephone message and he's *very angry.*
5. I wasn't invited to that party and I *don't care.*
6. It was only a small matter. Why are you *making it a big problem?*
7. He wears pink shirts with bright green pants. What an *eccentric character!*
8. She thinks she's the boss but she isn't. I think you better *remind her of that.*
9. I know that student hasn't been studying lately but the family has had personal problems. *Don't be drastic* in your punishment.

Lesson 66.   Turning the Tables

Dialogue
Ted: They **turned the tables** on him. He finally got **a dose of his own medicine.**
Will: I'm glad he **got what was coming to him.** Who **lowered the boom?** Did you **get to the bottom of** it?
Ted: Yes. It was his sister. She had the **backbone** to **stand up to him.**
Will: I'm glad she **started the ball rolling.** He'll have to be careful from now on.

Vocabulary

turn the tables	v.) reverse the situation
give someone a dose of his or her own medicine	v.) treat someone the same way he or she treats others
get what is coming to one	v.) get what one deserves—good or bad
lower the boom	v.) stop completely; punish strictly
get to the bottom of	v.) find out the real cause
backbone	n.) courage
stand up to someone	v.) be brave, courageously confront someone
start the ball rolling	v.) take the initiative, begin an action

Exercise I. *Complete the sentences with the correct idiom.*

a) started the ball rolling   b) a dose of his own medicine   c) turn the tables   d) got what was coming to him   e) stand up to   f) lowered the boom   g) backbone   h) get to the bottom of

1. We lost the game last night, but tonight we'll _____.
2. The big boy hit the small child. When the child's brother saw, he gave the big boy _____.
3. That man wanted to take her money. It was all she had left. She had to _____ him.
4. Nobody wanted to be the first to donate money to that charity so Harriet gave $100 and that _____.
5. The doctors had to take several tests to _____ the patient's complaints.
6. He'll do whatever anybody says. He has no _____.
7. When the father heard his children were not doing their homework, he _____.
8. He had a big test but did not study. He failed. He _____.

Exercise II. *Rewrite the phrases in italics, using the proper idiomatic expression.*

1. He wasn't making too much money last year but he worked hard and *reversed the situation*.
2. Let's *find out the real cause of* your headaches.
3. *Treat him the same way he treats you.*
4. This party is boring. Let's have some dancing. Who's going to *be the first?*
5. The child did something bad and now he's going to *be justly punished.*
6. If you don't like what he did, you have to *be brave and tell him.*
7. You're not going to be allowed to go out every night. Your father is going to *stop it completely.*
8. He's not a strong person. He has no *courage.*

Lesson 67. Mudslinging

Dialogue

Tracy: It's too bad his political opponents resorted to **mudslinging.** I hate to see someone **raked over the coals.**

Lola: They really **put him through the wringer.** They had the **gall** to **hit below the belt.**

Tracy: He won't **take it lying down.** He'll **go down swinging.**

Lola: You're right. He won't **say "uncle."**

Vocabulary

mudslinging	n.) making malicious remarks to damage someone's reputation
rake over the coals	v.) scold, reprimand, blame
put through the wringer	v.) cause severe stress
gall	n.) shameless, insolent attitude
hit below the belt	v.) hurt someone cruelly and unfairly
take something lying down	v.) suffer without a fight
go down swinging	v.) lose but fight until the end
say (cry) "uncle"	v.) admit defeat

Exercise I. *Complete the sentences with the correct idiom.*

a) raked him over the coals   b) hitting below the belt   c) mudslinging   d) gall   e) take that lying down   f) put through the wringer   g) went down swinging   h) said "uncle"

1. He wasn't going to lose easily. He fought all the way. He _____.
2. We had him down on the ground and wouldn't let him up until he _____.
3. He was not doing a good job so his boss _____.
4. The politician implied that his opponent's family was dishonest. Everyone agreed he was _____.
5. Her husband just had an operation. By the time it was over, she had been _____.
6. She spent all her money on clothes and records, then she asked to borrow money for groceries. She has _____.
7. She worked very hard for a promotion. One of her colleagues was jealous and mentioned she had been an alcoholic. That was _____.
8. Someone said he was dishonest. He's not going to _____.

Exercise II. *Rewrite the phrases in italics, using the proper idiomatic expression.*

1. He won't *admit he lost.*
2. It's not right to resort to *malicious gossip about someone.*
3. Even though he lost, he *fought to the end.*
4. Because he was late all the time, the boss *reprimanded him.*
5. He is not going to *endure this misfortune without fighting back.*
6. Her child had a very bad accident. Until she was all right, the mother was *under terrible stress.*
7. She is not a very nice person. At times she can *be unfair and hurt people.*
8. He never picks up a check. Everyone else pays. He has *no shame.*

Lesson 68.   A Road Hog

Dialogue

Florence: Why is he such a **backseat driver** when he rides with me?
George: Because you're a **road hog.**
Florence: **Come off it.**
George: It's true. Everyone honks his horn at you. **In nothing flat,** you could be **side-swiped.**
Florence: I never **smacked into** anyone or had a **fender-bender.**
George: You're lucky your car hasn't been **totalled.**
Florence: You said **a mouthful.**

Vocabulary

backseat driver	n.) passenger who tells you how to drive
road hog	n.) person who takes too much room on the road
Come off it.	Stop kidding, boasting or making believe.
in nothing flat	adv.) quickly, in a short time
side-swipe	v.) hit the side of a car
smack into	v.) collide, hit
fender-bender	n.) dent in the fender; minor accident
total	v.) completely ruin
a mouthful	n.) a true and impressive statement

Exercise I. *Complete the sentences with the correct idiom.*

a) smacked into   b) in nothing flat   c) road hog   d) side-swiped   e) totalled   f) fender-bender
g) backseat driver   h) come off it   i) he said a mouthful

1. There was a terrible accident. The car went into a telephone pole. It was _____.
2. My wife tells me how to drive. She's a _____.
3. I didn't stop at a stop sign and somebody _____ me.
4. He drives all over the road. He's a _____.
5. The road was icy and there were many _____.
6. Arthur said he was the only one who could do the job. I told him to _____.
7. When he heard I was taking him out for dinner, he got dressed _____.
8. The road was so narrow that when the truck passed, my car was _____.
9. My boss said I needed a vacation. He's right! _____.

Exercise II. *Rewrite the phrases in italics, using the proper idiomatic expression.*
1. He was driving carelessly and *completely ruined* his car.
2. He was backing up and *hit* the tree.
3. He ate his dinner *very quickly.*
4. *He drives like he's the only one on the road.*
5. *She always tells everybody how to drive.*
6. *What you said was very true.*
7. You know that's not true. *Stop pretending.*
8. There wasn't too much damage when he was *hit on the side of his car.*
9. He hit another car. It was just a *minor collision.*

Lesson 69. A Blabbermouth

Dialogue

Alice: She **let the cat out of the bag.**
Millie: She's a **blabbermouth.**
Alice: She didn't mean to **blow the whistle** on him.
Millie: He's **fuming** anyway. He'll have **hard feelings** about this for a long time.
Alice: He **brought it on** himself. He **egged her on.**
Millie: Don't **dwell on** it. Maybe it will **blow over.**

Vocabulary

let the cat out of the bag	v.) tell a secret
blabbermouth	n.) person who tells secrets and talks a lot
blow the whistle	v.) expose, betray
fume	v.) be angry
hard feelings	n.) anger, bitterness
bring on	v.) cause, produce
egg someone on	v.) urge, excite, push
dwell on	v.) talk and think about something all the time
blow over	v.) end, pass

Exercise I. *Complete the sentences with the correct idiom.*

a) blabbermouth   b) blow over   c) hard feelings   d) fuming   e) blew the whistle   f) brought it on
g) egged him on   h) let the cat out of the bag   i) dwell on

1. She didn't tell me she was pregnant. Her husband _____.
2. She only talks about money. I wish she wouldn't _____ this subject all the time.
3. The child didn't want to take the candy but his friends kept urging him. They _____.
4. He never saved any money. When he needed it he didn't have any. He _____ himself.
5. She saw who robbed the store and told the police. She _____ on him.
6. Somebody stole my money. I'm _____.
7. She talks so much. She's a _____.
8. Everyone is talking about the scandal in her family. She hopes it will _____ soon.
9. We hated each other as children, but today there are no _____ between us.

Exercise II. *Rewrite the phrases in italics, using the proper idiomatic expression.*

1. She *talks too much.*
2. I'm *angry.*
3. Don't *think about it all the time.*
4. By mistake, I *told the secret.*
5. Don't keep *urging him and pushing him* to do something wrong.
6. She was the only one who knew his whereabouts. The police wanted him, and she *betrayed him.*
7. Careless spending will *result in* inflation.
8. Let's not have any *anger* between us.
9. After her grandfather died, she was depressed. But this will *pass.*

Lesson 70. A Bookworm

Dialogue

Irene: I don't want to **hold you up.** I see you're **in a rush.**
Kate: If I don't get to work soon, I'll be **in the doghouse.** My job is a **pain in the neck.**
Irene: You're a **bookworm.** Why don't you go back to school?
Kate: I should **look into** it. What do you think I should **take up?**
Irene: That's **up to you.** Pick a job where you can make a lot of money.
Kate: Maybe computer science would **do the trick.**

Vocabulary

hold up   v.) delay, postpone
in a rush   adj. or adv.) in a hurry
in the doghouse   adj.) in trouble
pain in the neck   n.) bothersome, annoying thing or person
bookworm   n.) person who reads a lot
look into   v.) investigate, check
take up   v.) begin an activity or hobby
up to someone   n.) someone's choice
do the trick   v.) be successful, achieve a good result

Exercise I. *Complete the sentences with the correct idiom.*

a) take up   b) in a rush   c) held me up   d) look into   e) bookworm   f) did the trick   g) up to   h) in the doghouse   i) pain in the neck

1. He reads a lot. He's a _____.
2. Taking out the garbage is a _____.
3. I lost all my money. When I get home I'll be _____.
4. Do you believe she wants to _____ karate?
5. The phone was ringing so much today. It _____.
6. Maybe I'll buy that insurance. Tomorrow I'll _____ it.
7. What movie do you want to see? It's _____ you.
8. She wanted to make her husband happy. She made his favorite meal. That _____.
9. I can't see anyone right now. I'm _____.

Exercise II. *Rewrite the phrases in italics, using the proper idiomatic expression.*

1. I could not get here earlier because I was *delayed.*
2. If she doesn't clean the house before her mother gets home, she'll be *in a lot of trouble.*
3. He is *always reading.*
4. I would like to *study* computers.
5. I don't want to be late. If I left ten minutes earlier, that should *get good results.*
6. Arthur is always *in a hurry* to catch his bus.
7. I don't care where we go tonight. It's *your choice.*
8. Before he got the job, the company *investigated* his background.
9. I've been trying to telephone her all day but the line is busy. That's *annoying.*

Lesson 71.   Use Your Noodle

Dialogue

Adam: I can't **figure out** why he's **buttering me up.**

Ken: You're right. It doesn't **make sense.** I'm **stuck** also.

Adam: Let's **read between the lines** and not **jump to conclusions.**

Ken: **Use your noodle.** Don't let him **take advantage of** you.

Vocabulary

figure out	v.) try to understand, solve
butter up	v.) flatter for selfish reasons
make sense	v.) be comprehensible
stuck	adj.) unable to understand, remember, or solve; unable to move
read between the lines	v.) understand things that are not said, find a hidden meaning
jump to conclusions	v.) make quick but unjustified conclusions
use one's noodle (head)	v.) think
take advantage of	v.) treat unfairly for your own gain; make good use of time or conditions

Exercise I. *Complete the sentences with the correct idiom.*

a) use your noodle   b) take advantage of   c) make sense   d) figure it out   e) jump to the conclusion
f) read between the lines   g) buttering me up   h) stuck

1. He is a very nice person. It's a shame that some people try to _____ him.
2. 3xy + 2x2 + 3yz ? I can't _____.
3. What's that word in English "rgldoq"? It doesn't _____.
4. I'm trying to remember your name but I can't. I'm _____.
5. Don't _____ that all well-dressed men are rich.
6. They say they are happily married but I think you have to _____.
7. I know you know the answer. Think some more—_____.
8. Why is he saying I'm so wonderful and terrific? He's _____.

Exercise II. *Rewrite the phrases in italics, using the proper idiomatic expression.*

1. The boss doesn't pay overtime. He *treats his employees very unfairly.*
2. Don't *make an unjustified decision* because he didn't keep his appointment.
3. Try to think of the answer. *Don't guess.*
4. That's not the real reason they're not getting married. We have to *understand things that are not said.*
5. I know him from somewhere but *I can't remember exactly.*
6. If someone explains it to me, I can *understand it.*
7. When he wants something, he *flatters you.*
8. My car has a flat tire. *I can't drive it.*

Lesson 72.   Putting Yourself Out

Dialogue
Len: You **go out of your way** for **every Tom, Dick and Harry. Once in a blue moon** you could **put yourself out** for your family.

Marty: Stop **finding fault with** me. I'll be there when you need me.

Len: Okay, then let's **get the show on the road** and I'll stop **bugging you.**

Marty: **Keep your shirt on.** I'll **give you a hand.**

Vocabulary

go out of one's way	v.) make a special effort, do more than necessary
every Tom, Dick and Harry	n.) the average person, nobody special
once in a blue moon	adv.) occasionally; rarely
put one out	v.) inconvenience, bother
find fault	v.) complain, criticize
get the show on the road	v.) start a project or work
bug	v.) annoy, bother
keep one's shirt on	v.) be patient, wait
give someone a hand	v.) help

Exercise I. *Complete the sentences with the correct idiom.*
a) every Tom, Dick and Harry   b) get the show on the road   c) goes out of her way   d) give me a hand
e) once in a blue moon   f) put you out   g) bug   h) finds fault   i) keep your shirt on

1. I don't like the movies. I go _____.
2. When you are invited to her house, she always serves a special dinner. She _____ to make you feel welcome.
3. Thank you for giving me a ride. I hope I didn't _____.
4. Her mother never thinks she looks right. She _____ with her.
5. I know it's taking me a long time to finish my work, but _____.
6. I'm busy. Don't _____ me.
7. We have a lot of work to do today. Let's _____.
8. This desk is too heavy to move. Please _____.
9. He's an unusual dresser. He doesn't want to look like _____.

Exercise II. *Rewrite the phrases in italics, using the proper idiomatic expression.*
1. Stop *bothering* me.
2. She always *tries very hard* to make you feel comfortable.
3. Would somebody *help me?*
4. Let's *start.*
5. I go to French restaurants *rarely.*
6. Please *be patient.*
7. She *complains about* everything.
8. I don't want to *inconvenience you.*
9. He doesn't want to be like *the average person.*

Lesson 73. The Lowdown

Dialogue

Mel: The TV news just **filled us in** on that story of political corruption. It **floored me.**

Frank: Yes, that was some **earful.** What do you **make of it?**

Mel: It **crossed my mind** that the reporters have only **scratched the surface.** The politicians have denied everything.

Frank: Do you think we'll ever discover the real **lowdown?**

Mel: If we **bide our time,** I'm sure the reporters will **call the politicians' bluff.**

Vocabulary

fill someone in	v.) tell a person the details
floor someone	v.) surprise, confuse
earful	n.) especially interesting gossip, information
make of something	v.) interpret, figure out, think of
cross one's mind	v.) think of, occur quickly to someone
scratch the surface	v.) merely begin to understand or accomplish something
lowdown	n.) the true story
bide one's time	v.) wait patiently for the right opportunity
call someone's bluff	v.) challenge someone's empty threats, have someone prove what he says

Exercise I. *Complete the sentences with the correct idiom.*

a) scratched the surface   b) floored him   c) make of   d) fill me in   e) earful   f) crossed my mind
g) bide his time   h) call his bluff   i) lowdown

1. They were going to get married tomorrow but they cancelled their plans. What's the _____?
2. They were arguing and everyone could hear them. We got an _____.
3. I didn't read the paper today. Can you _____?
4. What do you _____ his decision to get a job and not go to college?
5. He didn't study very hard in that class so when he got an A, it _____.
6. I was going to ask him to join me for dinner but it _____ that he had to go out of town.
7. He wanted to ask for a raise but because business is a little slow, he's going to _____.
8. I don't think Bob knows as much as he says. I think we should _____.
9. I thought I knew a lot about Japanese history. Then I realized I had only _____.

Exercise II. *Rewrite the phrases in italics, using the proper idiomatic expression.*

1. I don't believe him. *Have him prove what he says.*
2. *Tell me all the details.*
3. I think you should *wait until you get the right chance.*
4. That really *surprised me.*
5. That sounds interesting. Tell me the *whole story.*
6. They didn't see me when they were arguing and I got *a lot of information.*
7. That's not even half the story. We have *a lot more to find out.*
8. What do you *think of* their idea?
9. That never *occurred to me.*

Lesson 74. A Heart-to-Heart Talk

Dialogue

Laura: I think it's about time we had a **heart-to-heart** talk. Why don't you **let your hair down?**

Tina: I'd like to **get something off my chest.** I think you could help me because you've **been around.**

Laura: **I'm all ears.** Don't **hold anything back.**

Tina: I won't **beat around the bush.** It's a long story so I'll **boil it down.**

Vocabulary

heart-to-heart	adj.) intimate, honest
let one's hair down	v.) be informal, relaxed
get something off one's chest	v.) unburden oneself; tell what's bothering you
have been around	v.) to be experienced, sophisticated
all ears	adj.) eager to listen
hold back	v.) conceal, hide
beat around the bush	v.) avoid giving a clear answer
boil down	v.) make shorter, condense

Exercise I. *Complete the sentences with the correct idiom.*

a) been around   b) beat around the bush   c) heart-to-heart   d) get it off my chest   e) hold something back   f) let your hair down   g) boil it down   h) all ears

1. It's been bothering me for a long time so I had to _____.
2. The girl was upset about her boyfriend, so her mother had a _____ talk with her.
3. It's always good to ask an older person's advice. He's usually _____.
4. I can't wait to hear that story. I'm _____.
5. He didn't tell me the whole story. Why did he _____?
6. Her story is so long. I wish she'd _____.
7. I don't understand what you mean. Give me a straight answer. Don't _____.
8. I like parties that are friendly and relaxed, where you can _____.

Exercise II. *Rewrite the phrases in italics, using the proper idiomatic expression.*

1. That was a long book, but when they made it into a TV movie, they *condensed it.*
2. I think we should *speak seriously.*
3. I'm glad you came over to visit. Come on in and *relax.*
4. Don't *conceal* any information.
5. He'd make an excellent ambassador. He's *experienced and worldly.*
6. *Would you please give me a clearer answer.*
7. I have to *tell you what's bothering me.*
8. How did your job interview go? *I can't wait to hear.*

Lesson 75. Wishy-Washy

Dialogue

Tony: He's a **wimp.** He has no **guts.**

Joan: You **took the words right out of my mouth.** He should **put his cards on the table.**

Tony: He's too **wishy-washy.** He's scared to **side with** anyone.

Joan: He won't **go to bat for** me either.

Tony: Be careful he doesn't **double-cross** you.

Joan: Don't worry. I won't be **left holding the bag.**

Vocabulary

wimp	n.) spineless, non-assertive person
guts	n.) courage
take the words out of someone's mouth	v.) say something someone else was going to say
put one's cards on the table	v.) be frank, tell everything
wishy-washy	adj.) having no definite opinion; unable to decide
side with	v.) favor, support one position in a dispute
go to bat for	v.) assist, help
double-cross	v.) betray
leave someone holding the bag	v.) put someone in an awkward position, leave someone else to take blame

Exercise I. *Complete the sentences with the correct idiom.*

a) took the words out of my mouth   b) go to bat for   c) wishy-washy   d) guts   e) put his cards on the table   f) left holding the bag   g) double-cross   h) wimp   i) side with

1. The children ate all the cookies and ran away. John stayed and he was _____.
2. I can rely on my friends. If I am in trouble, they will _____ me.
3. He betrayed me. I don't like people who _____ me.
4. He never tells you exactly what he wants. I think he should _____.
5. They're always fighting in front of me. I don't like it when they ask whom I _____.
6. He never has his own opinion. He's _____.
7. He's going to jump from a plane with a parachute. That takes _____.
8. I was just going to say he was a liar. You _____.
9. That type of person never speaks up for himself. He's a _____.

Exercise II. *Rewrite the phrases in italics, using the proper idiomatic expression.*

1. We all agreed to share the cost of the present, but I was *the only one who paid.*
2. If you have a problem at work, he'll always *help* you.
3. *He never has an opinion.*
4. He has *courage.*
5. He's a *weakling.*
6. *That's exactly what I was going to say.*
7. I don't understand what you're doing. Please *be frank.*
8. I always *sympathized with* her position in the divorce.
9. Why did she *betray* him?

Lesson 76.   Going to Pieces

Dialogue
Betty: I'm **at my wit's end.** My husband just **went under the knife** for cancer.
Edith: **Snap out of it.** Don't **go to pieces.**
Betty: Why are the doctors **in a huddle?** Did he **go from bad to worse?** Do you think he'll **pass away?**
Edith: He'll be **out of the woods** soon. Just **keep a stiff upper lip.**

Vocabulary
at one's wit's end	adj.) frantic, anxious; not knowing what to do next
go under the knife	v.) have surgery
go to pieces	v.) become crazy, hysterical; lose control of oneself
snap out of it	v.) free oneself from the control of panic, fear, hysteria, etc.
in a huddle	adj.) conferring confidentially
go from bad to worse	v.) deteriorate
pass away	v.) die
out of the woods	adj.) no longer in danger, in the clear
keep a stiff upper lip	v.) have courage, be brave

Exercise I. *Complete the sentences with the correct idiom.*
a) keep a stiff upper lip   b) goes under the knife   c) out of the woods   d) snaps out of it   e) at her wit's end   f) passed away   g) in a huddle   h) went from bad to worse   i) went to pieces

1. He's been in a terrible mood all day. I hope he _____.
2. I was sorry to hear that you lost your job. Don't worry, you'll find one soon. Just _____.
3. She couldn't find her child in the supermarket. She was _____.
4. She's in the hospital with a serious disease. I think she _____ tomorrow.
5. I didn't know he was 98 years old. He was a very nice man. I was sorry to hear he

   _____.
6. When the police called and said her son was in a bad accident, she _____.
7. Their marriage was never really any good, but I see it has deteriorated. It _____.
8. They're together discussing plans for the party. I feel left out when they're all _____.
9. The baby had a high fever for three days, but I'm happy to hear he's now _____.

Exercise II. *Rewrite the phrases in italics, using the proper idiomatic expression.*
1. The football team is *confidentially discussing the next play.*
2. He is *no longer in any danger.*
3. *Be brave.*
4. She *went crazy* when her child got hurt.
5. When did he *have surgery?*
6. You're in a bad mood. *Change it.*
7. I know he hasn't been feeling very well, but his condition has *deteriorated.*
8. I was sorry to hear he *died.*
9. He has three exams in one day. He's *frantic.*

Lesson 77.   Hold Your Horses

Dialogue

Paul: **Hold your horses.**

Dan: I can't. I have **ants in my pants.**

Paul: Try not to worry. Maybe he'll let you **off the hook.** Maybe it **slipped his mind.**

Dan: That sounds **far-fetched** to me, but I'd be **tickled pink.**

Paul: I don't think there's a problem. You're talking about **chickenfeed.**

Dan: Not to him. He's a **tightwad.** He'll want to get paid **come hell or high water.**

Vocabulary

hold one's horses	v.) wait
ants in one's pants	n.) nervousness, anxiety
off the hook	adj. or adv.) out of trouble, freed from an embarrassing situation
slip one's mind	v.) be forgotten
far-fetched	adj.) exaggerated, unlikely
tickled pink	adj.) very happy
chickenfeed	n.) a small amount of money
tightwad	n.) person who is cheap and stingy
come hell or high water	adv.) no matter what happens

Exercise I. *Complete the sentences with the correct idiom.*

a) chickenfeed   b) come hell or high water   c) hold your horses   d) tightwad   e) ants in their pants
f) off the hook   g) tickled pink   h) far-fetched   i) slipped my mind

1. He never spends money in a restaurant. He's a _____.
2. I can't leave the office yet. I'm waiting for an important phone call. Just _____.
3. The children can't wait to have candy. They have _____.
4. I don't want to have dinner at their house. If I tell them I'm going on a business trip, maybe that will get me _____.
5. They just found out they were going to be parents. They are _____.
6. He only earns a small amount of money each week. It's _____.
7. Tina loves her job so much that she'll go to work _____.
8. That is a crazy story. It sounds _____ to me.
9. I'm sorry I forgot to call. It _____.

Exercise II. *Rewrite the phrases in italics, using the proper idiomatic expression.*

1. He is *so cheap.*
2. She just got engaged. She's *so happy.*
3. You're not getting any candy before dinner, *no matter what you do.*
4. I can't speak to you right now. Just *wait.*
5. He had two appointments for one night. If one would cancel, he'd be *out of an embarrassing situation.*
6. Barbara is waiting for an important letter. She *is very anxious.*
7. Don't work for them. They pay *very little money.*
8. Most of Bob's stories were *exaggerated.*
9. *I didn't remember his birthday party.*

Lesson 78.   Through the Grapevine

Dialogue

Rose: I didn't know my assistant was **two-faced**. He **stabbed me in the back**.
Carol: I wouldn't **put anything past** him. How were you **tipped off?**
Rose: I heard it **through the grapevine**. I could **kick myself** for confiding in him.
Carol: I hope you **sailed into** him.
Rose: Not only will I **tell him off,** but I'm going to **give him his walking papers.**

Vocabulary

two-faced	adj.) disloyal, untrustworthy
stab someone in the back	v.) betray someone
put anything past someone (neg.)	v.) be surprised by what someone does
tip someone off	v.) warn, inform
through the grapevine	adv.) via gossip from other people
kick oneself	v.) regret, be sorry for
sail into	v.) get angry verbally
tell someone off	v.) speak to angrily
give someone his or her walking papers	v.) dismiss, fire; send away

Exercise I. *Complete the sentences with the correct idiom.*

a) tell him off   b) through the grapevine   c) sail into   d) walking papers   e) tipped off   f) stabbed him in the back   g) kick himself   h) two-faced   i) put anything past her

1. He promised my boss a lot of business, but he gave the business to someone else. He _____.
2. He could _____ for not buying property 10 years ago. He could have made a fortune.
3. The burglars were arrested because the police were _____.
4. She didn't tell me she was pregnant. I heard it _____.
5. Whenever an employee is found stealing, he is given his _____.
6. Whenever he gets too arrogant it's necessary to _____.
7. If your child is disrespectful, it's time to _____ him.
8. She'll tell you that you have a beautiful dress but when you leave, she'll say you're too fat to wear that style. She's _____.
9. She would lie to her own mother. I wouldn't _____.

Exercise II. *Rewrite the phrases in italics, using the proper idiomatic expression.*

1. She didn't like the way her boyfriend was acting, so she *ended the relationship*.
2. *I regret* I never got a college education.
3. I heard *from other people* that he was quitting his job.
4. He was an hour late and his boss *spoke to him angrily*.
5. He was told he got a promotion, but they *gave it to someone else instead*.
6. You must be careful around him. He is *untrustworthy*.
7. I knew they were giving me a surprise birthday because someone *told me* yesterday.
8. They said he stole money. I wouldn't *be surprised by anything he does*.
9. The child brought home a bad report and the parents *yelled at him*.

Lesson 79.   On the Q.T.

Dialogue
Sheila: This project is **hush-hush**. Don't **breathe a word** because we don't want anyone **upsetting the applecart**.

Carl: I know we can **put our heads together** only **on the q.t.,** but I wish it could be **above board**.

Sheila: Just stop **hassling** me. **Put it out of your head** for now. If anyone finds out, we'll be **in Dutch**.

Vocabulary

hush-hush	adj.) secret
breathe a word (neg.)	v.) tell, talk
upset the applecart	v.) ruin or spoil a plan or idea
put our heads together	v.) confer, discuss
on the q.t.	adv.) secretly
above board	adj.) open, legitimate, legal
hassle	v.) bother
put something out of one's head (mind)	v.) try not to think about
in Dutch	adj.) in trouble

Exercise I. *Complete the sentences with the correct idiom.*
a) put it out of your head   b) upset the applecart   c) on the q.t.   d) hassle   e) putting our heads together   f) breathe a word   g) hush-hush   h) in Dutch   i) above board

1. They don't want anyone to know and they'll only talk about it _____.
2. He's very trustworthy. If you don't want anyone to know, I'm sure he won't _____.
3. She doesn't want anyone to know about her engagement, so keep it _____.
4. Our plans are perfect. Don't discuss it with anyone. We don't want to _____.
5. I don't want to keep my plans secret. I want everything _____.
6. This project is giving us a lot of problems. Let's solve it by _____.
7. We are not going to spend any more money, so just _____.
8. Your brother has a lot of studying to do. He can't help you fix your car so don't _____ him.
9. If you don't get home to do your chores, you're going to be _____.

Exercise II. *Rewrite the phrases in italics, using the proper idiomatic expression.*
1. You're not going to fail that exam. *Don't think about it anymore.*
2. Everything should be *out in the open.*
3. Please don't tell anybody. It's *a secret.*
4. I think we should *all discuss it.*
5. Don't *tell anybody.*
6. He's going to be *in trouble.*
7. They have been seeing each other *secretly.*
8. He doesn't want you to *bother* him.
9. He's going to *ruin our plans.*

Lesson 80.   A Quack

Dialogue

Mae: That doctor is a **quack.** You **run a risk** if you use him.
Susan: He won't talk **straight from the shoulder.** He thinks I believe him **hook, line and sinker.**
Mae: Don't have him **pull any punches.** Ask him if it's a **touch and go** situation.
Susan: You're right. I'm **sick and tired** of getting the **runaround.**
Mae: As far as I'm concerned, he's nothing but **hot air.**

Vocabulary

quack	n.) an ignorant or fraudulent doctor
run (take) a risk	v.) be open to danger or loss, unprotected
straight from the shoulder	adv.) open and honest way of speaking
hook, line and sinker	adv.) without question or doubt
pull punches	v.) hide unpleasant facts or make them seem good
touch and go	adj.) very dangerous or uncertain
sick and tired	adj.) disliking some continual behavior, annoyed
get (give) the runaround	v.) be sent from place to place without getting the information needed
hot air	n.) nonsense or exaggerated talk

Exercise I. *Complete the sentences with the correct idiom.*
a) touch and go   b) hot air   c) runaround   d) straight from the shoulder   e) quack   f) pull any punches   g) sick and tired   h) run a risk   i) hook, line and sinker

1. You _____ of being hit by a car if you cross the street without looking.
2. He spoke bluntly. He didn't _____.
3. What did I do wrong? Tell it to me _____.
4. That doctor is no good. He's a _____.
5. The salesman said the car was in good condition. The customer believed him _____.
6. Don't listen to him. He doesn't know anything. It's a lot of _____.
7. The team won the game by a narrow margin. It was _____ for a while.
8. I'm _____ of eating hamburgers every day.
9. I was overcharged on my bill. Nobody wants to help. I keep getting the _____.

Exercise II. *Rewrite the phrases in italics, using the proper idiomatic expression.*
1. We don't know who's going to win that game. It's *a very uncertain outcome.*
2. That's a lot of *nonsense.*
3. They *sent me from place to place without giving me the information I needed.*
4. Tell him he better not *hide the truth.*
5. *The programs on television are continuously bad.*
6. That doctor *doesn't know what he's doing.*
7. I want you to *honestly give me your opinion.*
8. If you go out in the rain without an umbrella, you'll *probably catch a cold.*
9. I believed *everything he said.*

Lesson 81.   A Stuffed Shirt

Dialogue

Bryan: That new employee is **a stuffed shirt.** I **had his number** from the start.

Harold: You were right **all along.** Nobody can **break the ice** with him. He's **getting off on the wrong foot.**

Bryan: I think we'll have to **cut him down to size.**

Harold: When they chose him, they **scraped the bottom of the barrel.**

Bryan: He is **the pits.**

Harold: I think he got the job **by the skin of his teeth.**

Vocabulary

stuffed shirt   n.) a person who is rigid or too formal

have someone's number   v.) know what kind of person someone is

all along   adv.) all the time

break the ice   v.) overcome formality or shyness with others

get off (start off) on the wrong foot   v.) make a bad start

cut someone down to size   v.) prove someone is not as good as he or she thinks

scrape the bottom of the barrel   v.) take whatever is left after the best has been taken

the pits   n.) the worst, anything that is very bad

by the skin of one's teeth   adv.) by a very small margin

Exercise I. *Complete the sentences with the correct idiom.*

a) cut him down to size   b) all along   c) by the skin of his teeth   d) the pits   e) scrape the bottom
of the barrel   f) got off on the wrong foot   g) stuffed shirt   h) had his number   i) break the ice

1. I went to that new movie and it was awful. It was _____.
2. The vote was 102 to 100. He won _____.
3. He never smiles or has any fun. All he thinks about is doing things properly. He is a
   _____.
4. Ann chewed gum her first day at school and the teacher was angry. I think Ann _____.
5. It is difficult to find good soldiers. The Army has to _____.
6. On the first day of school, the new student kept answering all the teacher's questions. The other
   students _____.
7. The big boy tried to hit John but John knew karate and _____.
8. We won, but I knew we would _____.
9. When you don't know anyone at a party, it is hard to _____.

Exercise II. *Rewrite the phrases in italics, using the proper idiomatic expression.*

1. He won *by a very small margin.*
2. He is a *very stiff and rigid person.*
3. I *knew what kind of person he was.*
4. *He made a bad first impression.*
5. *All the time* he spoke English and I didn't realize it.
6. I didn't get the top workers so I have to *take whatever is left.*
7. He thinks he's so smart. We'll have to *show him he isn't.*
8. That party was *the worst.*
9. It is very difficult to *become friendly* with people you don't know.

Lesson 82.   The Bum's Rush

Dialogue

Adam: It didn't **dawn on me** that I was getting **the bum's rush.**
Zachary: If I were you, I'd make **a big stink.** Don't let him **bulldoze** you.
Adam: I don't want to **rock the boat.** Maybe I should **sleep on it.**
Zachary: No. He's **getting away with murder.** Say something now and **let the chips fall where they may.**

Vocabulary

dawn on	v.) become clear, begin to understand
the bum's rush	n.) rude, hurried treatment intended to get rid of someone quickly
a big stink	n.) an angry and loud complaint
bulldoze	v.) intimidate, coerce
rock the boat	v.) upset the status quo
sleep on it	v.) think about, consider, decide later
get away with murder	v.) not be punished for wrongdoing
Let the chips fall where they may.	Act regardless of consequences.

Exercise I. *Complete the sentences with the correct idiom.*

a) sleep on it   b) rock the boat   c) the bum's rush   d) bulldoze   e) a big stink   f) let the chips fall where they may   g) getting away with murder   h) dawned on

1. It's his wife's birthday today. He almost forgot. It just _____ him.
2. They weren't interested in buying insurance from him, so they gave him _____.
3. He wanted to know if she'd marry him but she said she'd let him know tomorrow. She had to _____.
4. He's having trouble with his marriage. If he has his mother move in, that would _____ even more.
5. He's so angry and the problem is so unimportant. I don't understand why he's making _____.
6. He's the boss's son, so if he comes in late everyday, you can't complain. He's _____.
7. The police were asking him questions about a robbery. He knew he had to tell them everything he saw and _____.
8. I know he's bigger than you but don't let him _____ you.

Exercise II. *Rewrite the phrases in italics, using the proper idiomatic expression.*

1. He *never gets punished when he does something wrong.*
2. *Finally I understand* what he means.
3. Don't let anyone *intimidate* you.
4. He *complained very loudly* about his new job.
5. I'm not too sure about my decision. I'll have to *think about it.*
6. *I don't know the outcome of this, but I have to do it anyway.*
7. I don't understand why they *got rid of me so quickly.*
8. They were angry when I *interfered* by asking questions about their policy.

Lesson 83. Barking Up the Wrong Tree

Dialogue
Bob: **Mum's the word.**

Mary: Don't worry. I won't **air your dirty linen in public.**

Bob: What are you **driving at?** I don't have any **skeletons in my closet.**

Mary: Maybe I'm **barking up the wrong tree** but I **felt it in my bones** that you were **covering for** someone.

Bob: That's **hogwash.**

Vocabulary

Mum's the word.	Don't talk about what was said.
air one's dirty linen (laundry) in public	v.) discuss personal problems indiscreetly
drive at	v.) try to say, insinuate
skeleton in one's closet	n.) a family secret
bark up the wrong tree	v.) make a wrong choice or false assumption
feel in one's bones	v.) feel certain without evidence, know by intuition
cover for someone	v.) protect someone
hogwash	n.) nonsense

Exercise I. *Complete the sentences with the correct idiom.*
a) was driving at   b) barking up the wrong tree   c) covered for him   d) air her dirty linen in public
e) mum's the word   f) feel it in my bones   g) hogwash   h) skeletons in their closet

1. I don't want anyone to know. _____.
2. The speech was so unclear. Nobody knew what he _____.
3. She's a quiet, private person. If there's a problem in her family, she doesn't want to _____.
4. I don't believe what he's saying. That's _____.
5. They're a family of many secrets. I bet there are _____.
6. I don't know why you keep asking him to lend you money. He doesn't have any. You're _____.
7. I know he's going to win that election by a landslide. I can _____.
8. He wasn't back from lunch yet but when the boss asked where he was his secretary said he was at a business meeting. She _____.

Exercise II. *Rewrite the phrases in italics, using the proper idiomatic expression.*
1. They're very strange. I think they have many *family secrets.*
2. *Don't tell anyone what I said.*
3. It's embarrassing to *discuss personal problems in public.*
4. If you asked him to fix your car, you *chose the wrong person.*
5. He says he doesn't want to go away on vacation. That's *nonsense.*
6. She didn't want him to get in trouble, so she *protected him.*
7. I don't understand you. What are you *trying to say?*
8. I don't care if they seem happy. I *can tell* that they fight all the time.

Lesson 84.   Getting Bombed

Dialogue
Mickey: I really got **bombed** last night.
Debbie: How come?
Mickey: Two of my closest friends **tied the knot** and there was **plenty of booze.**
Debbie: Did the bride and groom get **loaded** too?
Mickey: No. He's **on the wagon** and she's a **teetotaler.**
Debbie: I'm glad he's **staying away from** drinking.

Vocabulary
bombed	adj.) drunk
tie the knot	v.) get married
plenty of	adj.) a lot of, abundant
booze	n.) liquor
loaded	adj.) drunk
on the wagon	adj.) abstaining from liquor
teetotaler	n.) person who never drinks liquor
stay away from	v.) avoid

Exercise I. *Complete the sentences with the correct idiom.*
a) booze   b) loaded   c) bombed   d) plenty of   e) teetotaler   f) on the wagon   g) stay away from
h) tie the knot

1. They are in love and want to _____.
2. He can't drink any liquor. He's _____.
3. He had a lot to drink. He got _____.
4. There's a lot of _____ in a liquor store.
5. A person who is fat should _____ eating too much.
6. They drank a lot and were _____.
7. He doesn't drink liquor. He's a _____.
8. Rockefeller has _____ money.

Exercise II. *Rewrite the phrases in italics, using the proper idiomatic expression.*
1. He was *drunk.*
2. They *got married.*
3. There's *a lot of* food on the table.
4. What kind of *liquor* does he drink?
5. He got *drunk* last night.
6. *He doesn't drink liquor anymore.*
7. *She never drinks liquor.*
8. She *avoids* fattening foods.

Lesson 85.   A Clip Joint

Dialogue
Jessica: You didn't **miss out on** anything. That restaurant was some **clip joint.**
Cynthia: How did you hear about this **tourist trap—word of mouth?**
Jessica: No, I picked it **at random.**
Cynthia: How was the **chow?**
Jessica: Terrible. Worse than a **greasy spoon.** When I saw the check I nearly **passed out.**
Cynthia: Do you think they **padded the bill?**

Vocabulary
miss out on	v.) lose an opportunity, miss a worthwhile event
clip joint	n.) low-class nightclub or restaurant that overcharges people
tourist trap	n.) any place that is overpriced and attracts tourists
word of mouth	n.) recommendation from other people
at random	adv.) without order or plan, haphazardly
chow	n.) food
greasy spoon	n.) inexpensive restaurant with mediocre food
pass out	v.) faint
pad the bill	v.) add false expenses

Exercise I. *Complete the sentences with the correct idiom.*
a) word of mouth   b) padded the bill   c) tourist trap   d) at random   e) chow   f) miss out on   g) greasy spoon   h) clip joint   i) passed out

1. Everybody in the army hated the _____.
2. That restaurant was terrible. It was a _____.
3. They charged us for too many drinks. I think they _____.
4. Don't go to that terrible nightclub. They cheat you. It's a _____.
5. When I saw all that blood, I nearly _____.
6. I wanted to go to that party but I was sick. I had to _____ it.
7. They are very reputable and don't advertise. People know of it by _____.
8. He won a bicycle in the contest. They chose his name _____.
9. That nightclub has a famous name but its show is terrible and its food is expensive. It's a

_____.

Exercise II. *Rewrite the phrases in italics, using the proper idiomatic expression.*
1. I didn't buy that but they *charged me for it.*
2. That job is a great opportunity. I hope I don't *lose it.*
3. He *fainted.*
4. That nightclub *cheats people.*
5. That restaurant is *cheap, but the food is bad.*
6. That nightclub is *overpriced but it's popular with travelers.*
7. I'm hungry. Where's the *food?*
8. That restaurant was good. I ate there because of *a friend's recommendation.*
9. He opened his birthday presents *in no particular order.*

Lesson 86.   A Hit

Dialogue

Al: I heard that play was a big **flop** . . . a real **turkey.**
Lee: On the contrary, it's **a hit.**
Al: Do you think they're going to be **mobbed?**
Lee: **Jam-packed.** It's a **tearjerker.** You'll have to go to a **scalper** for tickets.
Al: Then let's buy the tickets two years **in advance.**
Lee: We may be **6 feet under** before we can see the show.

Vocabulary

flop/turkey   n.) failure
hit   n.) a success
mobbed   adj.) crowded
jam-packed   adj.) crowded, full
tearjerker   n.) story that makes you cry
scalper   n.) a person who buys a ticket at the regular rate and sells it at a profit
in advance   adv.) ahead of time
6 feet under   adj.) dead

Exercise I. *Complete the sentences with the correct idiom.*
a) a hit   b) mobbed   c) a tearjerker   d) a flop   e) a scalper   f) in advance   g) 6 feet under
h) jam-packed

1. During Christmas, the stores are _____.
2. If you continue to drink and smoke a lot, you'll be _____.
3. Doctors are so busy you have to make an appointment _____.
4. That movie was so sad. It was _____.
5. I want a ticket to that show so badly. I'll pay anything. I'll go to _____.
6. Every day the subways are _____.
7. Everyone is buying that record. It's _____.
8. He wrote a book but no one bought it. It was _____.

Exercise II. *Rewrite the phrases in italics, using the proper idiomatic expression.*
1. That show was *not a success.*
2. *There are a lot of people in the stores at Christmas time.*
3. The book is *very successful.*
4. That movie *made me cry.*
5. *That man makes a living selling concert tickets at twice their value.*
6. If you want to eat in that restaurant, you need reservations *ahead of time.*
7. I won't stop eating candy until I'm *dead.*

Lesson 87. A Nightcap

Dialogue

Tad: Do you want to go to a **gin mill** for a **pick-me-up?**
Doug: Yeah. Maybe if I **wet my whistle**, I'll **perk up**.
Tad: A **nightcap** would **hit the spot**.
Doug: Will I have to **shell out** much money?
Tad: Don't worry. I'll **lay it out**.

Vocabulary

a gin mill	n.) a cheap bar or nightclub
a pick-me-up	n.) a drink or snack taken to refresh oneself
wet one's whistle	v.) have a drink, especially alcohol
perk up	v.) emerge from a depressed or uninterested mood
a nightcap	n.) last drink one has before leaving or sleeping
hit the spot	v.) refresh or satisfy
shell out	v.) pay
lay out	v.) spend or pay

Exercise I. *Complete the sentences with the correct idiom.*

a) a nightcap   b) hit the spot   c) shell out   d) wet my whistle   e) lay it out   f) gin mills   g) a pick-me-up   h) perk up

1. I don't have enough money with me to buy that blouse. Do you think you could _____ for me?
2. In factory districts, _____ can usually be found on every corner.
3. I'm so thirsty. I'd like to _____.
4. When you come in from shoveling snow, a hot chocolate will usually _____.
5. Stop being in such a bad mood. If we go out, you'll _____.
6. When some people are tense and can't sleep at night, they sometimes have _____.
7. I worked very hard today and I'm tired. I think I need _____.
8. I made a lot of long distance calls last month. I'm going to have to _____ a lot of money.

Exercise II. *Rewrite the phrases in italics, using the proper idiomatic expression.*

1. I was so dirty from working in the garden. That shower *refreshed me.*
2. When you are employed by a fast-food restaurant, you must *pay for* uniforms.
3. I had such a tiring day. I need a *drink.*
4. The construction workers went to the bar after work to *have a drink.*
5. I feel tired. A cold shower will *make me feel better.*
6. I was tense today. I think I'll have *a drink before going to sleep.*
7. We went out for dinner but instead of choosing a fine restaurant, we mistakenly went into *a cheap nightclub.*
8. If you don't have enough money for dinner, I'll *pay.*

Lesson 88. Spine-Chilling

Dialogue

Mickey: I was **on the edge of my seat.** That movie was **spine-chilling.**
David: Everyone got **bumped off.** It gave me **the creeps.**
Mickey: It **shook me up** too. I still have **the jitters.**
David: Did you guess who **knocked everyone off?** I **caught on** right away.
Mickey: No. I had **ruled out** the real murderer.

Vocabulary

on the edge of one's seat	adj.) in nervous suspense
spine-chilling	adj.) terrifying, thrilling
bump off	v.) kill
the creeps	n.) revulsion, fear, uneasiness
shook up	adj.) upset, worried, fearful
the jitters	n.) anxiety, nervousness
knock off	v.) kill, leave, stop
catch on	v.) understand, figure out
rule out	v.) decide against, eliminate

Exercise I. *Complete the sentences with the correct idiom.*

a) spine-chilling   b) shook up   c) on the edge of my seat   d) bumped off   e) the creeps   f) knock off
g) the jitters   h) rule out   i) caught on

1. That story was so exciting, I was _____.
2. I was in the bank when the robbers came in. It was _____.
3. Everyone was surprised to hear the leader of the gang was _____.
4. That old house gives me _____.
5. After the accident, I was _____.
6. Before I take any test, I get _____.
7. Math was difficult until I had a great teacher. After she explained everything, I _____.
8. I have an important date tonight. I think I'll _____ work a couple of hours early.
9. He has to learn a language in school. He doesn't want to be a doctor or priest, so we can _____ Latin.

Exercise II. *Rewrite the phrases in italics, using the proper idiomatic expression.*

1. It was a very exciting football game and we were *in constant suspense.*
2. I tried very hard to explain it. I hope he *understood.*
3. *He makes me uneasy.*
4. After her husband died, she was very *upset.*
5. He wants to go on vacation but he's afraid to fly. I think Australia would be *an unlikely choice.*
6. He's not in the office now. He *left* a couple of hours earlier.
7. Before I speak in front of an audience, I have *a lot of anxiety.*
8. The police *killed* the gangster.
9. That movie was *terrifying.*

Lesson 89. On the House

Dialogue

John: Do you know these drinks are **on the house?**
Sue: Who's **the sport?**
John: The boss. He's **bending over backward** to **make a go of** the business. He feels if he **springs** now, later he'll be **on easy street.**
Sue: Well, he bought this place **for a song** and it'll be **a gold mine.**

Vocabulary

on the house	adj.) provided free by a bar or restaurant
sport	n.) person generous with money
bend over backward	v.) try very hard, make a great effort
make a go of	v.) succeed, produce good results
spring	v.) pay
on easy street	adv.) having a pleasant, secure life
for a song	adv.) at a low price, cheap
a gold mine	n.) worth a lot of money, successful

Exercise I. *Complete the sentences with the correct idiom.*

a) for a song   b) on the house   c) bend over backward   d) easy street   e) spring   f) sport   g) gold mine   h) make a go of

1. She didn't care how expensive that dress was. She was going to _____ for it.
2. He made a lot of money. Now he's on _____.
3. She was giving a very important dinner party and was going to _____ to make the evening a success.
4. He was married before but this time he plans to _____ his marriage.
5. That house was very cheap. He bought it _____.
6. When he takes a girl out he goes to the best restaurants, buys her flowers and rents a limousine. He's a _____.
7. He bought all the customers a drink. The drinks were _____.
8. That new restaurant is always busy. They make a lot of money. It's a _____.

Exercise II. *Rewrite the phrases in italics, using the proper idiomatic expression.*

1. She bought that property *when it was very cheap.*
2. Because they're working so hard on their business, I'm sure *they will succeed.*
3. Because he was not satisfied with his meal, the restaurant owner told him *he didn't have to pay.*
4. When we go out, he always pays. He's *very generous.*
5. *I try very hard* to be pleasant to people.
6. I don't know if I should *buy* that very expensive dress even though I love it.
7. She worked very hard in the store and now it's *very successful.*
8. Her uncle died and left her a lot of money. Now *she is rich.*

Lesson 90.   A Has-Been

Dialogue
Julie: That performer is a **has-been**. He's been **washed up** for **ages**.
Bruce: I think he's going to **have a go at** a **comeback**. This time he'll **sink or swim**.
Julie: He doesn't have **what it takes**. I saw his act. It was **from hunger**.
Bruce: Then this will probably be his **swan song**.

Vocabulary
has-been	n.) person once popular but no longer in public favor
washed up	adj.) no longer successful or needed; failed
ages	n.) a long time
have a go at	v.) to try, often after others have failed
comeback	n.) an attempt to reclaim a respected position, be successful again
sink or swim	v.) fail or succeed by your own efforts
what it takes	n.) any ability for a job; courage
from hunger	adj.) terrible, bad
swan song	n.) final appearance

Exercise I. *Complete the sentences with the correct idiom.*
a) has-been   b) have a go at   c) from hunger   d) what it takes   e) ages   f) swan song   g) sink or swim   h) comeback   i) washed up

1. Nobody else could open the bottle but she wanted to _____ it.
2. She'll never perform after tonight. This is her _____.
3. Is that the beautiful dress you were talking about? I think it's terrible. It's strictly _____.
4. I'm alone in the office. I hope I don't make a bad mistake. Nobody can help me. It's _____.
5. She's a terrific mother. She has patience and love. She has _____.
6. She used to be a big star. I'd love to see her perform again. I hope she makes a _____.
7. I'm so happy you visited. I haven't seen you in _____.
8. His ideas are old-fashioned. He's _____.
9. A long time ago, she was a very beautiful model, but now she's a _____.

Exercise II. *Rewrite the phrases in italics, using the proper idiomatic expression.*
1. That meal was *terrible*.
2. Either I'm going *to fail or succeed*, but I'm going to try hard.
3. I know you couldn't do it, but let me *try*.
4. I haven't eaten apple pie in *such a long time*.
5. Once she was very popular, but now nobody knows her. She wants to *be famous again*.
6. He was popular 20 years ago, but now *nobody remembers him*.
7. *The mayor's career is finished* because he was dishonest.
8. You should hire her for the job. She has *a lot of experience and ability*.
9. She doesn't want to be in show business anymore. This is her *final appearance*.

Lesson 91.   Knocking One for a Loop

Dialogue
Donna: How did you like the movie? I hear it **raised a lot of eyebrows.**
Harold: **In a nutshell,** it was not my **cup of tea.**
Donna: It wasn't **up my alley** either. It **knocked me for a loop.** I was **ill at ease.**
Harold: You should have **flown the coop.** I'm surprised you **stuck it out.**
Donna: I should never have gone. I would have **called it off** but I was with a group of people.

Vocabulary
raise eyebrows	v.) cause surprise or disapproval, shock
in a nutshell	adv.) briefly
one's cup of tea (neg.)	n.) something one enjoys, special interest
up one's alley	adj.) something one enjoys, special interest
knock one for a loop	v.) surprise
ill at ease	adj.) uncomfortable
fly the coop	v.) leave suddenly, run away
stick it out	v.) endure, continue
call off	v.) cancel

Exercise I. *Complete the sentences with the correct idiom.*
a) in a nutshell   b) stick it out   c) ill at ease   d) flown the coop   e) raised eyebrows   f) up your alley
g) my cup of tea   h) called off

1. I don't like sports, so bowling is not _____.
2. I could tell you about my vacation for hours, but _____ I had a great time.
3. I'm shy, so when I go to a cocktail party, I am _____.
4. His tooth was feeling better, so he _____ his dentist appointment.
5. It was 5 o'clock and most of the employees had already _____.
6. He doesn't like his job but he needs the money. He can't quit. He must _____.
7. I'm going to the Museum of Art on Sunday. I know you love to paint, so this is _____.
8. When she wore the bikini at the country club, it _____.

Exercise II. *Rewrite the phrases in italics, using the proper idiomatic expression.*
1. Tell me *briefly* what the meeting was about.
2. He had an appointment so he *left work suddenly.*
3. I know you don't like school, but a good education is important. You will have to *continue enduring it.*
4. You are not feeling well. *Cancel* your dinner date.
5. I am very *uncomfortable* when I meet new people.
6. If you love museums, a vacation in New York City would be *of special interest to you.*
7. Her choice of clothing *met with disapproval.*
8. Science fiction books *don't interest me.*

Lesson 92.   Ripped Off

Dialogue
Debbie: Why are you **down in the dumps?**
Mike: I bought some **hot** merchandise and got **ripped off.** The man **conned** me and I **fell for** it.
Debbie: **You're kidding!** Why can't you **size people up?**
Mike: I guess I'm still **wet behind the ears.** I fall for any **snow job.**

Vocabulary
down in the dumps	adj.) unhappy
hot	adj.) stolen (also means "in great demand": he's the **hottest** actor in town)
rip off	v.) cheat, rob
con	v.) lie, swindle, trick
fall for	v.) believe a false story
You're kidding!	Really? Is it true?
size up	v.) form an opinion, assess
wet behind the ears	adj.) inexperienced
snow job	n.) insincere or exaggerated talk intended to trick or impress

Exercise I. *Complete the sentences with the correct idiom.*
a) size him up   b) fell for it   c) conned   d) hot   e) snow job   f) You're kidding!   g) ripped off   h) down in the dumps   i) wet behind the ears

1. Joe didn't do any work all day but he told his boss he had been working very hard. He gave him a _____ .
2. I lost all my money. That's why I am _____ .
3. The used-car salesman _____ the man. He told him the car was in excellent shape.
4. When you meet someone for the first time, you usually _____ .
5. He told me he was a millionaire and I _____ .
6. I paid too much for those boots. I saw them cheaper in another store. I was _____ .
7. Don't buy that watch. It's stolen. It's _____ .
8. You found $1,000 in the street? _____ .
9. He can't manage the office; he's still _____ .

Exercise II. *Rewrite the phrases in italics, using the proper idiomatic expression.*
1. She lost her job. Now she is *unhappy*.
2. That watch is *stolen*.
3. I thought I bought a diamond but it was glass. I was *cheated*.
4. The salesman told me it was a good car, but the transmission was bad. He *tricked* me.
5. You're getting married? *Is it really true?*
6. How did you *assess* his qualifications?
7. You can tell him anything. He'll *believe* your story.
8. I wouldn't have gotten the job with the truth, so I gave him *an exaggerated story*.
9. She *doesn't have enough experience*.

Lesson 93.   A Grease Monkey

Dialogue

Robert: I heard he was a great **grease monkey.** How did he **make out?**

Mary: I asked him to give my car the **once-over.** You're right. He does have the **know-how.**

Robert: Some auto repairs are **rackets.** Just be careful he doesn't **pull a fast one.**

Mary: **Over my dead body.** I asked him to **point everything out.** I never let the situation **get out of hand.**

Vocabulary

grease monkey	n.) automobile mechanic
make out	v.) do, progress, succeed
once-over	n.) a quick look or examination
know-how	n.) experience and knowledge
racket	n.) easy, well-paying job; business that cheats customers
pull a fast one	v.) cheat, deceive
over one's dead body	adv.) under no condition, never
point out	v.) explain, show, call attention to
get out of hand	v.) lose control

Exercise I. *Complete the sentences with the correct idiom.*

a) make out   b) point out   c) over my dead body   d) getting out of hand   e) once-over   f) racket
g) grease monkey   h) pull a fast one   i) know-how

1. At first he drank liquor only at parties, but now he drinks every chance he gets. It's
_____.

2. She has a very easy job. She gets paid for doing almost nothing. What a _____.

3. When girls learn to cook, they usually rely on their mothers' _____.

4. I heard you went for a job interview. How did you _____?

5. He's very good at fixing cars. He'll be a good _____.

6. I don't trust that used-car salesman. He'll try to _____.

7. I work six days a week. Only _____ will I work on Sunday too.

8. When she walks down the street, the men give her the _____.

9. I asked her to _____ her house.

Exercise II. *Rewrite the phrases in italics, using the proper idiomatic expression.*

1. *Were you successful?*
2. Did you know he was *an auto mechanic?*
3. At first he only smoked a couple of cigarettes a day. Now he smokes two packs. It is *out of control.*
4. Don't buy any diamonds through mail advertisements. They *cheat customers.*
5. Her fiance just gave her a three-carat diamond ring. Of course everybody *looked at it.*
6. Don't try to do that yourself. *You're not experienced enough.*
7. He got paid for more overtime than he was entitled to. I don't like to say this, but I think he *deceived them.*
8. You must study. *Under no condition* can you go to a party on a school night.
9. She doesn't realize she's making an error. I'll have to *explain it* to her.

Lesson 94.   Free-for-All

Dialogue
Helen: It's a **free-for-all** in the stores during the Christmas holidays.
Laura: All merchandise **sells like hotcakes.** But some stores **jack up** the price.
Helen: Some stores have to be **on guard** because a lot of people have **sticky fingers.**
Laura: If someone enters a store with an oversized coat, the guards know it's not **kosher.**
Helen: When **shoplifters** are caught, I wonder if they **serve time.**
Laura: No. They usually **beat the rap.**

Vocabulary
free-for-all	n.) mayhem, disorder
sell like hotcakes	v.) sell quickly, rapidly
jack up	v.) raise prices
on guard	adj.) careful, wary
have sticky fingers	v.) be a thief
kosher	adj.) true, authentic, right
shoplifter	n.) one who steals goods from stores
serve time (do time)	v.) be in jail
beat the rap	v.) escape punishment

Exercise I. *Complete the sentences with the correct idiom.*
a) beat the rap   b) on guard   c) sticky fingers   d) kosher   e) free-for-all   f) jacked up   g) selling like hotcakes   h) serve time   i) shoplifter

1. That new record is a big hit. It's _____.
2. When that movie star was in town, all the women came to see him. It was a _____.
3. Because there was freezing weather in Florida, the price of oranges is going to be _____.
4. It's a very important meeting and we must think before we speak. We must be _____.
5. Don't leave money around. Someone here has _____.
6. He's selling 14 karat gold watches for $100. That doesn't sound _____.
7. When he was younger, he committed a crime. He had to _____ for two years.
8. He killed that man but because it was self-defense, he didn't have to go to jail. He _____.
9. Watch out for that woman when she comes into the store. She is a _____.

Exercise II. *Rewrite the phrases in italics, using the proper idiomatic expression.*
1. Did he ever *go to jail?*
2. I didn't know she *stole things.*
3. Let's buy a lot of them before they *raise* the prices.
4. That meeting was not organized. It was *very disorderly.*
5. I was surprised he *escaped punishment.*
6. I don't believe that story. It doesn't sound *authentic* to me.
7. Children always have to be *careful* when they speak to strangers.
8. Videocassette machines are selling *very rapidly.*
9. *He's a thief who only steals little items in department stores.*

Lesson 95. Putting Two and Two Together

Dialogue

Joyce: It's a shame you don't have any **horse sense. Right off the bat** you should have **put two and two together.**

Todd: You don't **miss a trick.** I can't believe I didn't **see through him.** I didn't think there were any **strings attached.**

Joyce: Well, it was a **close shave.** You better make sure nobody else **pulls the wool over your eyes.**

Vocabulary

horse sense	n.) practical intelligence
right off the bat	adv.) in the beginning, immediately
put two and two together	v.) make a conclusion knowing the facts
miss a trick (neg.)	v.) take advantage of every situation
see through	v.) understand the true character of someone or something
strings attached	n.) restraining circumstances, obligations
close shave	n.) narrow escape
pull the wool over one's eyes	v.) deceive, mislead

Exercise I. *Complete the sentences with the correct idiom.*

a) saw through him   b) close shave   c) pulled the wool over my eyes   d) horse sense   e) right off the bat   f) put two and two together   g) strings attached   h) doesn't miss a trick

1. I'm a good judge of character. I knew he was an honorable person _____.
2. I was really fooled. He _____.
3. He became company president but he had to marry the boss's daughter. There were

    _____.
4. She took her bathing suit and a picnic lunch so they _____ and knew that she was not going to work.
5. As soon as the boss left, she ran to the phone to make personal calls. She _____.
6. Everyone knew he was dishonest, I'm glad you finally _____.
7. She doesn't have a college education, but she's very knowledgeable. She has _____.
8. I nearly got hit by that car. That was a _____.

Exercise II. *Rewrite the phrases in italics, using the proper idiomatic expression.*

1. I think he *misleads her.*
2. If you are going to give me a promotion, I must have a free hand. There can be no *hidden obligations.*
3. *She can take advantage of any situation.*
4. *He immediately knew* that he was not going to like the class.
5. He *is a very practical person.*
6. As soon as she knows the facts, she'll *come to a conclusion.*
7. She *won't be fooled by his false image.*
8. I had a *narrow escape* at the beach. I almost drowned.

Lesson 96.   The Real McCoy

Dialogue

Mike: I'm **in a bind.** This man had some jewelry. He said if I bought **the whole kit and caboodle,** I could have it for **peanuts.**

Eric: I can't believe you didn't **smell a rat.**

Mike: At first I said, **no dice,** but he said he was selling it so cheap because he was in a **tight squeeze.**

Eric: Let me guess. The jewelry he **palmed off** wasn't the **real McCoy.** He left you **high and dry.**

Vocabulary

in a bind	adv.) in trouble no matter what you do
kit and caboodle	n.) the entire amount, all
peanuts	n.) a small amount of money
smell a rat	v.) become suspicious
No dice.	No. Certainly not.
tight squeeze	n.) difficult situation financially
real McCoy	n.) the genuine thing
palm off	v.) sell or get rid of by trickery
high and dry	adv. or adj.) alone without help, stranded

Exercise I. *Complete the sentences with the correct idiom.*

a) the real McCoy   b) in a bind   c) tight squeeze   d) high and dry   e) no dice   f) peanuts   g) palmed it off   h) smelled a rat   i) kit and caboodle

1. I'll take everything. Give me the whole _____.
2. I need to earn more money. What I'm making is _____.
3. After everybody left the party, I had to clean up by myself. I was left _____.
4. This ring only cost me $5.00. It isn't _____.
5. That car wasn't working right. The salesman _____ on me.
6. I like living in this area. When the children asked me to move south, I said, _____.
7. I don't have the money for that now. I'm in a _____.
8. I have a test tomorrow. Not only did I leave my notes at school, but I'm sick and don't feel well enough to study. I'm _____.
9. Somebody offered me expensive merchandise for a small amount of money. Of course I _____.

Exercise II. *Rewrite the phrases in italics, using the proper idiomatic expression.*

1. Everybody left me *alone* with all this work.
2. *I refuse to do that.*
3. I can understand why you *became suspicious.*
4. That company pays *very little money.*
5. I have a big problem. *No matter what I do, I'm in trouble.*
6. I'll buy *everything you have.*
7. I can't buy that now. *I'm short of money.*
8. I don't think that diamond is *genuine.*
9. I didn't want to buy that but he *tricked me.*

Lesson 97.   A Scam

Dialogue

Roger: You were some **chump** to believe that **scam.**

Carol: He **set me up** by telling me a **sob story.**

Roger: Didn't it sound **fishy** to you?

Carol: No. Nothing **rang a bell.** They just **pulled a number on** me.

Roger: Well, you only lost a couple of hundred **bucks.**

Carol: **That's nothing to sneeze at.**

Vocabulary

chump	n.) one who is easily fooled
scam	n.) a plan to cheat someone
set someone up	v.) put someone in a position to be manipulated
sob story	n.) sad story that makes the listener sympathetic
fishy	adj.) suspicious, false-sounding
ring a bell	v.) remind one of something familiar
pull a number on	v.) cheat, deceive
buck	n.) dollar
nothing to sneeze at	n.) something not trivial, to be taken seriously

Exercise I. *Complete the sentences with the correct idiom.*

a) that was nothing to sneeze at   b) ring a bell   c) chump   d) set me up   e) pulled a number on
f) sob story   g) fishy   h) bucks   i) scam

1. He believes what anybody tells him. He's a _____.
2. He was disappointed when he got a $1,000 bonus, but I told him _____.
3. He delivers papers after school and makes a couple of extra _____ a week.
4. Don't be surprised if she tells you about the tragedy in her family. It's some _____.
5. He told his mother he couldn't get home because he had a flat tire. That sounds _____.
6. I'm sure you met him before. Doesn't his name _____?
7. He told me his family needed money very badly and they had to sell some family jewels. I bought a gold ring but it wasn't real gold. He _____ me.
8. Sometimes an opportunity to make a lot of money sounds good, but it could be a _____.
9. I didn't realize I was being cheated. They carefully _____.

Exercise II. *Rewrite the phrases in italics, using the proper idiomatic expression.*

1. I don't think you realize that what you said is *very important.*
2. Does that *sound familiar?*
3. Whenever she's late for work, she gives the boss a *sad excuse.*
4. That was a *plan to cheat him.*
5. *You can fool him very easily.*
6. They *manipulated him* so that they could easily cheat him.
7. That story is *unbelievable.*
8. I think they are trying to *deceive* you.
9. That dress costs a hundred *dollars.*

Lesson 98.   A Raw Deal

Dialogue

Nick: I heard the judge **threw the book at him.**

Ernie: He should have **taken the Fifth.** Now they'll probably **send him up the river.**

Nick: I don't think he **had it coming.** They should **let him off.**

Ernie: He fought **tooth and nail,** but they **had him over a barrel.**

Nick: I think he got a **raw deal.**

Vocabulary

throw the book at	v.) punish severely for breaking rules or the law
take the Fifth	v.) refuse to testify against oneself, as guaranteed by the Fifth Amendment to the Constitution
up the river	adv.) in jail
have it coming	v.) deserve a punishment
let someone off	v.) excuse from a penalty or promise, permit to leave
tooth and nail	adv.) as hard as possible, fiercely
over a barrel	adv.) in a helpless, trapped position
raw deal	n.) unfair treatment

Exercise I. *Complete the sentences with the correct idiom.*

a) up the river   b) had me over a barrel   c) throw the book at me   d) took the Fifth   e) raw deal
f) had it coming   g) let him off   h) tooth and nail

1. He worked for that company for 15 years. They discharged him without notice. He got a

   _____.

2. He worked very hard. His success did not come easy. He fought _____.
3. If you commit a crime, you'll be sent _____.
4. Some people speed all the time and never get caught, but if I were caught speeding, they would

   _____.

5. He asked the fat girl how much she weighed. She was embarrassed and _____.
6. The teacher is punishing him because he fell asleep in class. She didn't realize he was sick. I think
   she should _____.
7. I didn't study for the examination and I failed. I _____.
8. He saw me cash my paycheck and then asked me for a loan. I could not refuse. He

   _____.

Exercise II. *Rewrite the phrases in italics, using the proper idiomatic expression.*

1. I can't believe he got such *unfair treatment.*
2. Did you realize he was *in jail?*
3. I'm *in a very difficult position.*
4. They *gave him a severe penalty.*
5. He *refused to answer that question.*
6. He fought *very hard* for everything he got.
7. The criminal *got a just punishment.*
8. All right. You don't have to do homework tonight. I'll *excuse you.*

Lesson 99. Getting the Ax

Dialogue
Arthur: **Keep this under your hat.** I just **pulled the rug out from under** the bartender.

Richard: **Cue me in** on what happened.

Arthur: He is **getting the ax** because he not only **watered down** the drinks but he **had his hand in the till.** I'm going to **send him packing.**

Richard: Nobody can **put anything over on you.**

Vocabulary
keep something under one's hat — v.) keep something secret

pull the rug out from under — v.) spoil someone's plans, withdraw support

cue someone in — v.) explain

get the ax — v.) be fired

water down — v.) dilute

have one's hand in the till — v.) steal from one's employer

send someone packing — v.) tell someone to leave, dismiss

put something over on someone — v.) fool

Exercise I. *Complete the sentences with the correct idiom.*
a) get the ax   b) pulled the rug out from under   c) had his hand in the till   d) send him packing

e) keep it under your hat   f) water it down   g) cue me in   h) put something over on

1. She doesn't want anyone to know she's getting married, so please _____.
2. This coffee is too strong. I think you should _____.
3. I think you got more information about the robbery than I did, so _____ on it.
4. Their marriage has been bad for a long time. They're always fighting. I think she's going to

   _____.
5. I didn't realize they were giving me a surprise party. They really _____ me.
6. The boss trusted the bartender and never realized he _____.
7. He has been a very bad employee for a long time. I'm surprised he didn't _____ long ago.
8. He was supposed to leave for Europe tomorrow but the airline strike _____ him.

Exercise II. *Rewrite the phrases in italics, using the proper idiomatic expression.*
1. He is getting a promotion, but *don't tell anyone about it yet.*
2. They found out he was dishonest. *He'll be dismissed.*
3. It's difficult for him to make plans because somebody always *spoils them.*
4. I don't have all the facts. *Tell me all you know.*
5. Were you aware that he *was stealing money from the business?*
6. You can't *fool him.*
7. *Tell him to leave.*
8. The drinks were *not strong.*

Lesson 100.   By Hook or by Crook

Dialogue
Bill: He wanted that merchandise **by hook or by crook.** He thought he could steal it, but he **had another guess coming.**

Fred: He never **kept his nose clean.** I am glad you finally **caught him red-handed.**

Bill: When I caught him, he should have **felt like two cents,** but he didn't **bat an eyelash.**

Fred: It's about time his **goose was cooked.** Now he'll have to **face the music.**

Vocabulary
by hook or by crook	adv.) by any means necessary
have another guess (think) coming	v.) be mistaken
keep one's nose clean	v.) stay out of trouble
catch someone red-handed	v.) find someone in the act of doing wrong
feel like two cents	v.) feel ashamed or embarrassed
bat an eyelash (neg.)	v.) show emotion
cook someone's goose	v.) create big problems for someone
face the music	v.) meet one's punishment, accept the consequences

Exercise I. *Complete the sentences with the correct idiom.*
a) caught him red-handed   b) kept his nose clean   c) goose is cooked   d) bat an eyelash   e) felt like two cents   f) have another guess coming   g) by hook or by crook   h) face the music

1. My boss is going to be angry. I was supposed to go to the bank, but I forgot about it. My _____.

2. There is no way I'm going to eat this terrible food. If you think I am, you _____.

3. After he was released from prison, he stayed out of trouble. His parents were glad he _____.

4. His mother overheard my unkind remarks. I _____.

5. I caught him lying but it didn't bother him. He didn't _____.

6. He wants to succeed so badly, he'll do it_____.

7. The child was not allowed to have cookies before dinner but his mother saw him taking some. She _____.

8. The teacher caught her cheating on the test. Now she has to _____.

Exercise II. *Rewrite the phrases in italics, using the proper idiomatic expression.*
1. When the teacher caught him cheating, he didn't *show any emotion.*
2. The police got the burglars *when they were robbing the bank.*
3. If you think I am going out on a cold night, you *are mistaken.*
4. The teenager used the family car without permission and had an accident. Now he's going home to *confront his parents' anger.*
5. He was going to be successful *any way he could.*
6. The main thing to remember is, *stay out of trouble.*
7. When she didn't receive an invitation to an important party, she *was embarrassed.*
8. I forgot to make an important phone call at work. The boss is going to be very angry. *I'm in trouble.*

ANSWERS TO EXERCISES

Lesson 1. Having a Ball
I: 1. d 2. c 3. h 4. b 5. f 6. a/e 7. g 8. e/a
II: 1. freeload 2. treat 3. go Dutch 4. splurge 5. I'm always loaded 6. picked up the tab 7. have a ball 8. I'm broke

Lesson 2. Footing the Bill
I: 1. e 2. a 3. f 4. c 5. h 6. d 7. g 8. b
II: 1. ran out of 2. pick up 3. fed up with 4. foot the bill 5. down the drain 6. chip in 7. odds and ends 8. Skip it!

Lesson 3. Making Ends Meet
I: 1. a 2. f 3. h 4. e 5. b 6. g 7. c 8. d
II: 1. shopping around 2. sky-high 3. great 4. made ends meet 5. cut corners 6. cut down on 7. a clotheshorse 8. dress up

Lesson 4. Raking It In
I: 1. g 2. d 3. e 4. c 5. a 6. b 7. f 8. h
II: 1. has it made 2. is a sore loser 3. making a bundle 4. rakes it in 5. hit the ceiling 6. took him to the cleaners 7. lost his shirt 8. He's a good sport

Lesson 5. Caught Short
I: 1. d 2. c 3. a 4. b 5. e 6. h 7. g 8. f
II: 1. brown bagging it 2. does without 3. feel sorry for 4. was caught short 5. in the chips 6. get along 7. tighten my belt 8. Money burns a hole in his pocket.

Lesson 6. An Arm and a Leg
I: 1. i 2. f 3. g 4. a 5. b 6. h 7. c 8. e/d
II: 1. grand/that ain't hay 2. jalopies 3. an arm and a leg 4. I'm in the market for 5. in a pinch 6. for the time being 7. A-1 8. set him back

Lesson 7. A Nest Egg
I: 1. d 2. e 3. a 4. h 5. c 6. f 7. b 8. g
II: 1. made a killing 2. squawk about 3. on pins and needles 4. She wants to keep up with the Joneses 5. a nest egg 6. bank on 7. All the work in his office is on his shoulders. 8. salted away

Lesson 8. Falling Behind
I: 1. d 2. b 3. c 4. i 5. f 6. h 7. g 8. e 9. a
II: 1. clears 2. flew off the handle 3. go over 4. tide you over 5. face up to 6. bounced 7. to the hilt 8. breaking her neck 9. I fall behind.

Lesson 9. When the Chips Are Down
I: 1. i 2. f 3. g 4. b 5. h 6. e 7. c 8. d 9. a
II: 1. sit tight 2. mooch 3. handouts 4. when the chips were down 5. down and out 6. They live hand to mouth. 7. He's a penny pincher. 8. turn to 9. get out from under

Lesson 10. Keeping One's Head Above Wa
I: 1. e 2. d 3. c 4. g 5. i 6. a 7. f 8. h 9. b
II: 1. keeping her head above water/back on 2. bail him out 3. he will see daylight 4. hard up 5. racking my brains 6. a drop in the bucket 7. moola 8. She puts up a good front.

Lesson 11. One for the Books
I: 1. f 2. a 3. h 4. e 5. b 6. d 7. g 8. c
II: 1. I had egg on my face. 2. have to take it with a grain of salt 3. a piece of cake/a cinch 4. a piece of cake/a cinch 5. one for the books 6. a nitwit 7. talking through his hat 8. half-baked

Lesson 12. An Eager Beaver
I: 1. d 2. f 3. a 4. b 5. c 6. h 7. e 8. g
II: 1. an eager beaver 2. count on 3. get ahead 4. goofs off 5. pitch in 6. crop up 7. a clockwatcher 8. guy

Lesson 13. Bringing Home the Bacon
I: 1. d 2. b 3. a 4. h 5. c 6. f 7. g 8. i 9. e
II: 1. I'm under the weather. 2. I'm swamped with work. 3. bring home the bacon 4. they're sitting pretty 5. spilled the beans 6. played hooky 7. hang in there 8. no picnic 9. in the long run

Lesson 14. On a Shoestring
I: 1. h 2. g 3. f 4. e 5. a 6. c 7. b 8. d
II: 1. on a shoestring 2. been through the mill 3. wind up 4. took a beating 5. out of the blue 6. a feather in the cap 7. strike while the iron is hot 8. well-heeled

Lesson 15. A Pep Talk
I: 1. e 2. g 3. c 4. b 5. h 6. a 7. d 8. f 9. i
II: 1. gung ho 2. clamp down 3. Let it ride 4. get around to 5. shaped up 6. a peptalk 7. off the record 8. in his shoes 9. give him a pink slip

Lesson 16. In Seventh Heaven
I: 1. e 2. c 3. h 4. a 5. g 6. f 7. i 8. b 9. d
II: 1. I'm keeping my fingers crossed. 2. stick to my guns 3. I mean business 4. made a hit 5. in seventh heaven 6. My head is in the clouds. 7. knocked him dead 8. hand it to her 9. it didn't pan out

Lesson 17. A Brainstorm
I: 1. h 2. e 3. f 4. d 5. b 6. c 7. g 8. a
II: 1. thought up 2. take the plunge 3. jump the gun 4. try out products 5. brainstorm 6. gets off the ground 7. take over 8. kick it around

Lesson 18. The Cream of the Crop
I: 1. a 2. h 3. b 4. e 5. f 6. g 7. c 8. d
II: 1. in the bag 2. a brain 3. cream of the crop 4. keeps her nose to the grindstone 5. has his feet on the ground

rubs me the wrong way 7. can't stand 8. She's always on the ball.

Lesson 19. Pulling Strings
I: 1. f 2. b 3. h 4. d 5. a/e 6. c 7. a 8. g
II: 1. He made his own way. 2. put in his two cents 3. to a T 4. pull some strings/throw his weight around 5. throw his weight around 6. big shot 7. his hands are tied 8. you're wasting your breath

Lesson 20. In the Swing of Things
I: 1. f 2. d 3. g 4. h 5. e 6. a 7. c 8. b 9. i
II: 1. give me a break 2. pulling my leg 3. a breeze 4. looking up 5. get into the swing of things 6. works his fingers to the bone 7. cut out 8. learn the ropes 9. taking on

Lesson 21. A Hustler
I: 1. h 2. a 3. c 4. i 5. f 6. b 7. d 8. e 9. g
II: 1. He's a soft touch. 2. a cock and bull story 3. hand over fist 4. hustler 5. sharp 6. a snowball's chance in hell 7. put the bite on you 8. a fast buck 9. feathers his own nest

Lesson 22. High Off the Hog
I: 1. c 2. f 3. d 4. i 5. e 6. g 7. h 8. a 9. b
II: 1. live high off the hog 2. is a sweatshop 3. slinging hash 4. He's strapped. 5. land on his feet 6. let any grass grow under his feet 7. He's in there pitching. 8. not so hot 9. take a crack at it

Lesson 23. Getting Down to Brass Tacks
I: 1. d 2. h 3. f 4. a 5. g 6. c 7. e 8. b
II: 1. He's on the gravy train. 2. out of this world 3. nitty-gritty 4. I'm game. 5. get down to brass tacks 6. in dribs and drabs 7. He has something up his sleeve. 8. sink our teeth into

Lesson 24. Straight from the Horse's Mouth
I: 1. f 2. b 3. a 4. e 5. c 6. g 7. d
II: 1. got wind of 2. a pretty penny 3. get on the bandwagon 4. straight from the horse's mouth 5. get in on the ground floor 6. beat me to the punch 7. cleaned up

Lesson 25. Coming Through with Flying Colors
I: 1. c 2. e 3. b 4. h 5. g 6. a 7. f 8. d 9. i
II: 1. dropped out of high school 2. I came through with flying colors. 3. take the bull by the horns 4. get to first base 5. miss the boat 6. a pat on the back 7. cut out 8. sort of 9. kidding around

Lesson 26. The Black Sheep
I: 1. h 2. c 3. a 4. b 5. i 6. e 7. d 8. g 9. f
II: 1. black sheep of his family 2. batted a thousand 3. go-getter 4. come a long way 5. He has two strikes against him. 6. take your hat off to him 7. was from the wrong side of the tracks 8. has a head on his shoulders 9. to boot

Lesson 27. In a Jam
I: 1. c 2. h 3. f 4. a 5. i 6. e 7. b 8. g 9. d
II: 1. John Hancock 2. on the level 3. get out of 4. They're in the red. 5. That's a fly-by-night company. 6. double-check 7. chalked up 8. in a jam 9. end up

Lesson 28. On the Go
I: 1. b 2. i 3. c 4. f 5. h 6. e 7. g 8. a 9. d
II: 1. beat 2. murder 3. take you for a ride 4. for the birds 5. ran me ragged 6. really on the go 7. grab 40 winks 8. roped into 9. pay through the nose

Lesson 29. Raising Cain
I: 1. e 2. a 3. f 4. g 5. b 6. c 7. d 8. h
II: 1. hold a grudge 2. let on 3. fell through 4. raised Cain 5. back out of 6. He had his heart set on returning 7. In order to make it up to you 8. How did your speech turn out?

Lesson 30. Behind the 8-Ball
I: 1. f 2. e 3. g 4. h 5. a 6. b 7. d 8. c
II: 1. up to my ears in 2. no bed of roses 3. buckle down 4. canned 5. make a dent in 6. Mind your P's and Q's 7. off his rocker   8. behind the 8-Ball

Lesson 31. Jack-of-All-Trades
I: 1. d 2. c 3. h 4. a 5. b 6. i 7. f 8. g 9. e
II: 1. a top-notch 2. He's a bum. 3. sleazy 4. dive 5. hit the skids 6. a high-brow 7. tough breaks 8. to drown his sorrows 9. a jack-of-all-trades

Lesson 32. Out on a Limb
I: 1. f 2. b 3. c 4. h 5. g 6. a 7. d 8. e
II: 1. sticking his neck out 2. The coast is clear. 3. wash our hands of him/give him the slip 4. in the klink 5. blabbing 6. out on a limb 7. My heart was in my mouth. 8. Wash your hands of it.

Lesson 33. Twiddling One's Thumbs
I: 1. i 2. g 3. a 4. b 5. h 6. d 7. f 8. c 9. e
II: 1. a dime a dozen 2. threw in the towel 3. falls off 4. He's calling it quits. 5. broke the news 6. beside himself 7. twiddles her thumbs 8. what's the bottom line 9. stinks

Lesson 34. Play It By Ear
I: 1. i 2. d 3. g 4. h 5. a 6. e 7. c 8. f 9. b
II: 1. handle her with kid gloves 2. iron out 3. louse up my plans 4. butt in 5. I'll get my foot in the door 6. put your foot in it 7. They gave me the brush-off. 8. Play it by ear. 9. make sure

Lesson 35. Off the Top of One's Head
I: 1. g 2. d 3. f 4. a 5. h 6. b 7. c 8. e 9. i
II: 1. pulled it off 2. Off the top of my head 3. sweating bullets 4. knocked myself out 5. a prayer 6. He went over his apartment with a fine-tooth comb. 7. wing it 8. a snap 9. blew it

Lesson 36. The Rat Race
I: 1. e 2. d 3. c 4. a 5. f 6. i 7. h 8. g 9. b
II: 1. he kicked the bucket 2. talk turkey 3. That's a rat race. 4. He's at the end of his rope. 5. getting me down 6. came apart at the seams 7. sell yourself short 8. This is a dead-end job. 9. He'll get cold feet.

Lesson 37. Keyed Up
I: 1. g 2. e 3. f 4. b 5. d 6. h 7. c 8. a
II: 1. doesn't know if he's coming or going 2. keyed up 3. lost his marbles 4. Get a grip on yourself./Simmer down. 5. He's hyper. 6. He bit off more than he could chew. 7. running around in circles 8. get a grip on himself

Lesson 38. Pounding the Pavement
I: 1. b 2. e 3. f 4. d 5. g 6. a 7. h 8. c 9. i
II: 1. gave him the third degree 2. squealed 3. on the spot 4. pounding the pavement 5. shooting the breeze 6. get under my skin 7. come clean 8. up to here with 9. I don't have the heart to

Lesson 39. A Hard Nut to Crack
I: 1. d/e 2. h 3. f 4. c 5. b 6. g 7. a 8. d/e
II: 1. pulling up stakes 2. a hard nut to crack 3. make your hair stand on end 4. within reason 5. go overboard/get carried away 6. got carried away/went overboard 7. put my finger on/pinpoint 8. put my finger on/pinpoint

Lesson 40. Back to the Drawing Board
I: 1. a 2. e 3. f 4. d 5. b 6. g 7. h 8. c
II: 1. a goner 2. back to the drawing board 3. bombed 4. a ballpark figure 5. they went over big 6. square one 7. went up in smoke 8. from left field

Lesson 41. Passing the Buck
I: 1. b 2. a 3. c 4. e 5. d 6. h 7. f 8. i 9. g
II: 1. in black and white 2. He got up on the wrong side of the bed./ He's out of sorts. 3. botched up his career 4. out of sorts 5. a rough 6. passing the buck 7. way off base 8. a nincompoop 9. pins him down to

Lesson 42. A Song and Dance
I: 1. c 2. f 3. a 4. d 5. g 6. h 7. b 8. e 9. i
II: 1. haven't been up to par 2. standing on his own two feet 3. smooth things over 4. gave her a song and dance 5. called on the carpet 6. throw cold water on 7. shoots any new ideas I have full of holes 8. give it my best shot 9. crack down

Lesson 43. The Apple of One's Eye
I: 1. d 2. c 3. g 4. j 5. e 6. h 7. b 8. a 9. f 10. i
II: 1. is spoiled 2. in hot water 3. in stitches 4. the apple of her eye 5. give in 6. get a kick out of 7. a handful 8. hit the nail on the head 9. kid 10. Get a load of

Lesson 44. Keeping in Touch
I: 1. d 2. h 3. e 4. b 5. c 6. f 7. i 8. a 9. g
II: 1. She's tied down. 2. live it up 3. track him down 4. lost track of him 5. he's settled down 6. chewed the fat 7. came across him 8. keep in touch 9. She's in a rut.

Lesson 45. Hitting It Off
I: 1. g 2. h 3. b 4. e 5. a 6. c 7. d 8. f
II: 1. swell 2. down-to-earth 3. buddy-buddy 4. turns me off 5. the size of it 6. put me on 7. gave me the cold shoulder 8. hit it off

Lesson 46. A Chip Off the Old Block
I: 1. d 2. i 3. g 4. h 5. e 6. f 7. c 8. a 9. b
II: 1. takes after 2. named her son after him 3. well-off 4. go to the movies off and on 5. steer clear of 6. look down their noses at 7. He's nobody's fool. 8. She takes after her. 9. You're the spitting image of him.

Lesson 47. Seeing Eye to Eye
I: 1. g 2. h 3. c 4. f 5. b 6. e 7. a 8. d
II: 1. sticks up for 2. puts down 3. see eye to eye 4. at odds 5. put my foot down 6. gave her a piece of my mind 7. leads him around by the nose 8. don't you have a mind of your own

Lesson 48. On the Rocks
I: 1. d 2. a 3. g 4. h 5. e 6. f 7. b 8. c
II: 1. on the rocks 2. make the best of it 3. work it out 4. aren't on the same wavelength 5. a false alarm 6. on shaky ground 7. at fault 8. split up

Lesson 49. An Old Flame
I: 1. f 2. a 3. i 4. d 5. g 6. e 7. h 8. c 9. b
II: 1. We have a blind date tonight. 2. turned her down 3. old flame 4. make up your mind 5. fell for 6. pop the question 7. it hit her like a ton of bricks 8. going steady 9. play the field

Lesson 50. A Wet Blanket
I: 1. c 2. d 3. b 4. a 5. f 6. g 7. h 8. i 9. e
II: 1. yells bloody murder 2. dumped her 3. live wire 4. get up and go 5. He's a wet blanket. 6. He stood us up. 7. had a crush on 8. fix you up 9. put a damper on it

Lesson 51. A Knockout
I: 1. a 2. h 3. d 4. g 5. b 6. c/i 7. e 8. f 9. c/i
II: 1. She's at his beck and call. 2. puts her on a pedestal 3. nuts about 4. has him twisted around her little finger

5. playing with fire 6. leading her on to 7. knockout
8. play up to 9. He laid it on thick

Lesson 52. A Sourpuss
I: 1. b/i 2. d 3. h 4. g 5. c 6. b/i 7. e 8. a 9. f
II: 1. weigh your words 2. out of line 3. rules the
roost/wears the pants in the family 4. sourpuss 5. puts
up with 6. fix his wagon 7. keep tabs on 8. she wears
the pants/rules the roost 9. push you around

Lesson 53. A Lemon
I: 1. g 2. a 3. c 4. e 5. d 6. f 7. h 8. i 9. b
II: 1. is on the blink 2. He's handy. 3. is a lemon 4. all
thumbs 5. falls apart 6. cough up 7. dough 8. have a fit
9. scraping together money

Lesson 54. High and Low
I: 1. b 2. g 3. c 4. h 5. f 6. i 7. a 8. d 9. e
II: 1. scattering his toys around 2. hit the sack 3. turn
up 4. Straighten your desk out. 5. high and low 6. mess
7. piling up 8. a slob 9. right under my nose

Lesson 55. The Boob Tube
I: 1. c/d 2. f 3. g 4. a 5. b 6. e 7. h 8. c/d
II: 1. doctor it up 2. that idea bit the dust 3. went
haywire 4. the boob tube 5. I'm on my last legs. 6. It's
on the fritz. 7. He's fiddling around with that computer.
8. He can kiss that film goodbye.

Lesson 56. Sprucing Up
I: 1. b 2. a 3. f 4. c 5. j 6. h 7. g 8. e 9. i 10. d
II: 1. elbow room 2. scrounging around for 3. loot 4. stuff
5. spruce up 6. dig up 7. second-hand 8. from scratch
9. went to pot 10. hemmed in

Lesson 57. A Pad
I: 1. d 2. g 3. h 4. f 5. a 6. c 7. b 8. e
II: 1. turns my stomach 2. spic and span 3. run-down
4. something under the table 5. pad 6. on a wild goose
chase 7. elbow grease 8. topsy-turvy

Lesson 58. Hitting the Bottle
I: 1. f 2. c 3. a 4. g 5. d 6. e 7. b 8. h
II: 1. beef 2. patch things up 3. Go cold turkey.
4. hitting the bottle 5. will power 6. broke up 7. He's
turning over a new leaf. 8. keep on

Lesson 59. In the Same Boat
I: 1. f 2. c 3. g 4. e 5. b 6. h 7. d 8. a 9. i
II: 1. Knock it off. 2. Take a powder. 3. hounding me
4. I'm in the same boat 5. he calls the shots 6. Get off
my back. 7. He has a one-track mind. 8. draw the line
9. a nag

Lesson 60. A Pill
I: 1. c 2. d 3. e 4. h 5. f 6. g 7. a 8. b

II: 1. take to heart 2. a looney bin 3. split hairs/nitpick
4. drive me up a wall 5. pill 6. nitpicking/splitting hairs
7. His behavior doesn't sit right with me. 8. harping on

Lesson 61. Dishing It Out
I: 1. b 2. c 3. g 4. d 5. f 6. a 7. h 8. e
II: 1. He has a chip on his shoulder. 2. whistles a
different tune 3. bone to pick with them 4. What are
you getting at? 5. He's got my goat. 6. take it 7. dishes it
out 8. I want to clear the air.

Lesson 62. Settling the Score
I: 1. c 2. b 3. a 4. g 5. d/h 6. f 7. i 8. e 9. d/h
II: 1. man-to-man 2. get even/settle the score 3. Not on
your life. 4. wisecracks 5. made a monkey out of him
6. Let bygones be bygones. 7. settle the score/get even
8. have it out 9. flipped his lid

Lesson 63. The Last Straw
I: 1. g 2. f 3. c 4. d 5. h 6. e 7. a 8. b
II: 1. nip bad habits in the bud 2. the last straw 3. just
shrug it off 4. bury the hatchet 5. make waves 6. the
fur's going to fly 7. make a mountain out of a molehill
8. making fun of

Lesson 64. A Kick in the Pants
I: 1. e 2. a 3. b 4. d 5. h 6. g 7. f 8. c
II: 1. get the short end of the stick 2. knocking my head
against the wall 3. fair and square 4. jumping down
someone's throat 5. get a kick in the pants 6. It will
serve you right. 7. walk all over 8. rubbing it in

Lesson 65. A Bum Ticker
I: 1. b 2. e 3. d 4. f 5. g 6. h 7. a 8. i 9. c
II: 1. bawl him out 2. bum ticker 3. bite your tongue
4. on the warpath 5. don't give a hoot 6. making a
federal case out of it 7. a lulu 8. put her in her place
9. Don't do anything rash

Lesson 66. Turning the Tables
I: 1. c 2. b 3. e 4. a 5. h 6. g 7. f 8. d
II: 1. turned the tables 2. get to the bottom of 3. Give
him a dose of his own medicine. 4. start the ball rolling
5. get what's coming to him 6. stand up to him 7. lower
the boom 8. backbone

Lesson 67. Mudslinging
I: 1. g 2. h 3. a 4. b/c 5. f 6. d 7. b/c 8. e
II: 1. say "uncle" 2. mudslinging 3. went down swinging
4. raked him over the coals 5. take this lying down
6. put through the wringer 7. hit below the belt
8. gall

Lesson 68. A Road Hog
I: 1. e 2. g 3. a 4. c 5. f 6. h 7. b 8. d 9. i
II: 1. totalled 2. smacked into 3. in nothing flat 4. He's a

road hog. 5. She's a backseat driver. 6. You said a mouthful. 7. Come off it. 8. side-swiped 9. fender-bender

Lesson 69. A Blabbermouth
I: 1. h 2. i 3. g 4. f 5. e 6. d 7. a 8. b 9. c
II: 1. is a blabbermouth 2. fuming 3. dwell on it 4. let the cat out of the bag 5. egging him on 6. blew the whistle on him 7. bring on 8. hard feelings 9. blow over

Lesson 70. A Bookworm
I: 1. e 2. i 3. h 4. a 5. c 6. d 7. g 8. f 9. b
II: 1. held up 2. in the doghouse 3. a bookworm 4. take up 5. do the trick 6. in a rush 7. up to you 8. looked into 9. a pain in the neck

Lesson 71. Use Your Noodle
I: 1. b 2. d 3. c 4. h 5. e 6. f 7. a/d 8. g
II: 1. takes advantage of his employees 2. jump to a conclusion 3. Use your noodle./Figure it out. 4. read between the lines 5. I'm stuck/I can't figure it out 6. make sense of it/figure it out 7. butters you up 8. I'm stuck.

Lesson 72. Putting Yourself Out
I: 1. e 2. c 3. f 4. h 5. i 6. g 7. b 8. d 9. a
II: 1. bugging 2. goes out of her way 3. give me a hand 4. get the show on the road 5. once in a blue moon 6. keep your shirt on 7. finds fault with 8. put you out 9. every Tom, Dick and Harry

Lesson 73. The Lowdown
I: 1. i 2. e 3. d 4. c 5. b 6. f 7. g 8. h 9. a
II: 1. Call his bluff. 2. Give me the lowdown./Fill me in. 3. bide your time 4. floored me 5. lowdown 6. an earful 7. only scratched the surface 8. make of 9. crossed my mind

Lesson 74. A Heart-to-Heart Talk
I: 1. d 2. c 3. a 4. h 5. e 6. g 7. b 8. f
II: 1. boiled it down 2. have a heart-to-heart talk 3. let your hair down 4. hold back 5. been around 6. Don't beat around the bush. 7. get something off my chest 8. I'm all ears.

Lesson 75. Wishy-Washy
I: 1. f 2. b 3. g 4. e 5. i 6. c 7. d 8. a 9. h
II: 1. left holding the bag 2. go to bat for 3. He's wishy-washy. 4. guts 5. wimp 6. You took the words right out of my mouth. 7. put your cards on the table 8. sided with 9. double-cross

Lesson 76. Going to Pieces
I: 1. d 2. a 3. e 4. b 5. f 6. i 7. h 8. g 9. c
II: 1. in a huddle 2. out of the woods 3. Keep a stiff upper lip. 4. went to pieces 5. go under the knife

6. Snap out of it. 7. gone from bad to worse 8. passed away 9. at his wit's end

Lesson 77. Hold Your Horses
I: 1. d 2. c 3. e 4. f 5. g 6. a 7. b 8. h 9. i
II: 1. a tightwad 2. tickled pink 3. come hell or high water 4. hold your horses 5. off the hook 6. has ants in her pants 7. chickenfeed 8. far-fetched 9. His birthday party slipped my mind.

Lesson 78. Through the Grapevine
I: 1. f 2. g 3. e 4. b 5. d 6. a 7. c 8. h 9. i
II: 1. gave him his walking papers 2. I could kick myself because 3. through the grapevine 4. told him off 5. stabbed him in the back 6. two-faced 7. tipped me off 8. put anything past him 9. sailed into him

Lesson 79. On the Q.T.
I: 1. c 2. f 3. g 4. b 5. i 6. e 7. a 8. d 9. h
II: 1. Put it out of your head. 2. above board 3. hush-hush 4. put our heads together 5. breathe a word 6. in Dutch 7. on the q.t. 8. hassle 9. upset the applecart

Lesson 80. A Quack
I: 1. h 2. f 3. d 4. e 5. i 6. b 7. a 8. g 9. c
II: 1. touch and go 2. hot air 3. gave me the runaround 4. pull any punches 5. I'm sick and tired of the programs on television. 6. is a quack 7. talk straight from the shoulder 8. run a risk of catching a cold 9. him hook, line and sinker

Lesson 81. A Stuffed Shirt
I: 1. d 2. c 3. g 4. f 5. e 6. h 7. a 8. b 9. i
II: 1. by the skin of his teeth 2. stuffed shirt 3. had his number 4. He got off on the wrong foot. 5. All along 6. scrape the bottom of the barrel 7. cut him down to size 8. the pits 9. break the ice

Lesson 82. The Bum's Rush
I: 1. h 2. c 3. a 4. b 5. e 6. g 7. f 8. d
II: 1. gets away with murder 2. Finally it dawns on me 3. bulldoze 4. made a big stink 5. sleep on it 6. I have to let the chips fall where they may. 7. gave me the bum's rush 8. rocked the boat

Lesson 83. Barking Up the Wrong Tree
I: 1. e 2. a 3. d 4. g 5. h 6. b 7. f 8. c
II: 1. skeletons in their closet 2. Mum's the word. 3. air your dirty linen in public 4. were barking up the wrong tree 5. hogwash 6. covered up for him 7. driving at 8. can feel it in my bones

Lesson 84. Getting Bombed
I: 1. h 2. f 3. b/c 4. a 5. g 6. b/c 7. e 8. d
II: 1. loaded/bombed 2. tied the knot 3. plenty of

4. booze   5. loaded/bombed   6. He's on the wagon.
7. She's a teetotaler.   8. stays away from

Lesson 85. A Clip Joint
I: 1. e 2. g 3. b 4. h 5. i 6. f 7. a 8. d 9. c
II: 1. padded the bill 2. miss out on 3. passed out 4. is a
clip joint 5. a greasy spoon 6. a tourist trap 7. chow
8. word of mouth 9. at random

Lesson 86. A Hit
I: 1. b/h 2. g 3. f 4. c 5. e 6. b/h 7. a 8. d
II: 1. a flop 2. The stores are mobbed (jam-packed) at
Christmas time.   3. a hit 4. is a tearjerker 5. That man
is a scalper. 6. in advance   7. 6 feet under

Lesson 87. A Nightcap
I: 1. e 2. f 3. d 4. b 5. h 6. a 7. g 8. c
II: 1. perked me up/hit the spot 2. shell out for
3. pick-me-up   4. wet their whistles 5. hit the spot/perk
me up 6. a nightcap 7. a gin mill 8. lay it out.

Lesson 88. Spine-Chilling
I: 1. c 2. a 3. d 4. e/g 5. b 6. g 7. i 8. f 9. h
II: 1. on the edge of our seats 2. caught on 3. He gives
me the creeps./He gives me the jitters. 4. shook up
5. ruled out 6. knocked off   7. the jitters 8. bumped off
9. spine-chilling

Lesson 89. On the House
I: 1. e 2. d 3. c 4. h 5. a 6. f 7. b 8. g
II: 1. for a song 2. they will make a go of it 3. it was
on the house   4. a sport 5. I bend over backwards
6. spring for 7. a gold mine   8. she's on easy
street

Lesson 90. A Has-Been
I: 1. b 2. f 3. c 4. g 5. d 6. h 7. e 8. i 9. a
II: 1. from hunger 2. sink or swim 3. have a go at it
4. ages 5. make a comeback 6. he's a has-been 7. The
mayor is washed up 8. what it takes   9. swan song

Lesson 91. Knocking One for a Loop
I: 1. g 2. a 3. c 4. h 5. d 6. b 7. f 8. e
II: 1. in a nutshell 2. flew the coop 3. stick it out 4. Call
off   5. ill at ease 6. up your alley/your cup of tea
7. raised eyebrows   8. aren't my cup of tea/aren't up my
alley

Lesson 92. Ripped Off
I: 1. e 2. h 3. c 4. a 5. b 6. g 7. d 8. f 9. i
II: 1. down in the dumps 2. hot 3. ripped off 4. conned
5. You're kidding! 6. size up 7. fall for 8. a snow job 9. is
wet behind the ears

Lesson 93. A Grease Monkey
I: 1. d 2. f 3. i 4. a 5. g 6. h 7. c 8. e 9. b
II: 1. How did you make out? 2. a grease monkey
3. getting out of hand   4. are a racket 5. gave it the
once-over 6. You don't have the know-how. 7. pulled a
fast one on them 8. Over my dead body 9. point it out

Lesson 94. Free-for-All
I: 1. g 2. e 3. f 4. b 5. c 6. d 7. h 8. a 9. i
II: 1. serve time 2. had sticky fingers 3. jack up 4. a
free-for-all   5. beat the rap 6. kosher 7. on guard 8. like
hotcakes   9. He's a shoplifter.

Lesson 95. Putting Two and Two Together
I: 1. e 2. c 3. g 4. f 5. h 6. a 7. d 8. b
II: 1. pulls the wool over her eyes 2. strings attached
3. She doesn't miss a trick.   4. Right off the bat he knew
5. has horse sense   6. put two and two together 7. will
see through him 8. close shave

Lesson 96. The Real McCoy
I: 1. i 2. f 3. d 4. a 5. g 6. e 7. c 8. b 9. h
II: 1. high and dry 2. No dice.   3. smelled a rat
4. peanuts 5. I'm in a bind./I'm in a tight squeeze. 6. the
whole kit and caboodle 7. I'm in a bind./I'm in a tight
squeeze. 8. the real McCoy 9. palmed it off on me

Lesson 97. A Scam
I: 1. c 2. a 3. h 4. f 5. g 6. b 7. e 8. i 9. d
II: 1. nothing to sneeze at 2. ring a bell 3. sob story
4. scam   5. He's a chump. 6. set him up 7. fishy 8. pull a
number on 9. bucks

Lesson 98. A Raw Deal
I: 1. e 2. h 3. a 4. c 5. d 6. g 7. f 8. b
II: 1. a raw deal 2. up the river 3. over a barrel
4. threw the book at him 5. took the Fifth 6. tooth and
nail   7. had it coming 8. let you off

Lesson 99. Getting the Ax
I: 1. e 2. f 3. g 4. d 5. h 6. c 7. a 8. b
II: 1. keep it under your hat 2. They'll send him
packing./He'll get the ax. 3. pulls the rug out from
under him 4. Cue me in. 5. had his hand in the till
6. put something over on him 7. Send him packing.
8. watered down

Lesson 100. By Hook or by Crook
I: 1. c 2. f 3. b 4. e 5. d 6. g 7. a 8. h
II: 1. bat an eyelash 2. red-handed 3. have another guess
coming   4. face the music 5. by hook or by crook 6. keep
your nose clean   7. felt like two cents 8. My goose is
cooked.

Numbers in parentheses indicate the lesson in which the idiom is introduced.

above board   adj.) open, legitimate, legal (79)

ages   n.) a long time (90)

air one's dirty linen (laundry) in public   v.) discuss personal problems indiscreetly (83)

all along   adv.) all the time (81)

all ears   adj.) eager to listen (74)

all thumbs   adj.) can't fix things, clumsy (53)

an arm and a leg   n.) a large amount of money (6)

ants in one's pants   n.) nervousness, anxiety (77)

apple of one's eye   n.) someone special, usually a son or daughter (43)

at fault   adj.) responsible, to blame (48)

at odds   adj.) in disagreement (47)

at one's beck and call   adj.) always ready to do as ordered (51)

at one's wit's end   adj.) frantic, anxious; not knowing what to do next (76)

at random   adv.) without order or plan, haphazardly (85)

at the end of one's rope   adj.) desperate, with nowhere to turn (36)

A-1   adj.) excellent (6)

back on one's feet   adj.) financially independent or physically healthy again (10)

back out of   v.) withdraw, end an obligation or promise (29)

back to the drawing board   adv.) ready to start over, refine or rethink an idea (40)

backbone   n.) courage (66)

backseat driver   n.) passenger who tells you how to drive (68)

bail one out   v.) help (10)

ballpark figure   n.) approximate amount (40)

bank on   v.) count on, be sure of (7)

bark up the wrong tree   v.) make a wrong choice or false assumption (83)

bat a thousand   v.) have a perfect record, whether good or bad (26)

bat an eyelash (neg.)   v.) show emotion (100)

bawl out   v.) reprimand (65)

be beside one's self   v.) be very upset, nervous, frantic (33)

beat   adj.) tired, exhausted (28)

beat around the bush   v.) avoid giving a clear answer (74)

beat someone to the punch (draw)   v.) do something before someone else can (24)

beat the rap   v.) escape punishment (94)

beef   n.) complaint (58)

behind the 8-ball   adj.) in trouble (30)

bend over backward   v.) try very hard, make a great effort (89)

bide one's time   v.) wait patiently for the right opportunity (73)

big shot   n.) important person (19)

big stink, a   n.) an angry and loud complaint (82)

bite off more than one can chew   v.) try to do more than one can physically or mentally handle (37)

bite one's tongue   v.) keep oneself from speaking (65)

bite the dust   v.) die, disappear (55)

blab   v.) talk too much (32)

blabbermouth   n.) person who tells secrets and talks a lot (69)

black sheep   n.) a family member with a bad reputation (26)

blind date   n.) date arranged for two people who don't know each other (49)

blow it   v.) lose a chance, make a mistake, forget (35)

blow over   v.) end, pass (69)

blow the whistle   v.) expose, betray (69)

boil down   v.) make shorter, condense (74)

bomb   v.) fail, be unsuccessful (40)

bombed   adj.) drunk (84)

bone to pick with someone   n.) complaint, dispute, argument (61)

boob tube   n.) television set (55)

bookworm   n.) person who reads a lot (70)

booze   n.) liquor (84)

botch up   v.) make a big mistake, ruin (41)

bottom line   n.) end result, ultimate cause, deciding factor (33)

bounce   v.) not be acceptable because of insufficient funds in the bank (said of checks) (8)

brain   n.) intelligent person (18)

brainstorm   n.) very smart idea (17)

break one's neck   v.) try very hard (8)

break the ice   v.) overcome formality or shyness with others (81)

break the news   v.) tell a surprising fact (33)

break up   v.) separate (58)

breathe a word (neg.)   v.) tell, talk (79)

breeze, a   n.) easy (20)

bring home the bacon   v.) earn the family's income (13)

bring on   v.) cause, produce (69)

broke   adj.) having no money (1)

brown bag   v.) bring one's lunch from home (5)

buck   n.) dollar (97)

buckle down   v.) study or work very hard (30)

buddy-buddy   adj.) very friendly (45)

bug   v.) annoy, bother (72)

bulldoze   v.) intimidate, coerce (82)

bum   n.) worthless person (31)

bum ticker   n.) weak or diseased heart (65)

bump off   v.) kill (88)

bum's rush, the   n.) rude, hurried treatment intended to get rid of someone quickly (82)

burn a hole in one's pocket   v.) to be spent quickly (5)

bury the hatchet   v.) make peace, stop arguing (63)

butt in   v.) interfere (34)

butter up   v.) flatter for selfish reasons (71)

by hook or by crook   adv.) by any means necessary (100)

by the skin of one's teeth   adv.) by a very small margin (81)

call it quits   v.) stop, finish, quit (33)

call off   v.) cancel (91)

call on the carpet   v.) reprimand (42)

call someone's bluff   v.) challenge someone's empty threats, have someone prove what he says (73)

call the shots   v.) be in charge, give orders (59)

can   v.) fire, dismiss (30)

carried away   adj.) adversely influenced by strong emotions (39)

catch on   v.) understand, figure out (88)

catch someone red-handed   v.) find one in the act of doing wrong (100)

caught short   adj.) having an insufficient supply (especially of money) when needed (5)

chalk up   v.) record, score (27)

chew the fat   v.) chat, talk idly (44)

chickenfeed   n.) a small amount of money (77)

chip in   v.) contribute, give jointly (2)

chip off the old block   n.) child who looks or acts like his or her parent (46)

chip on one's shoulder   n.) quarrelsome attitude, quick to anger (61)

chow   n.) food (85)

chump   n.) one who is easily fooled (97)

cinch, a   n.) easy (11)

clamp down   v.) become stricter (15)

clean up   v.) make a big profit (24)

clear   v.) go through, meet the requirements (8)

clear the air   v.) calm anger and remove misunderstanding (61)

clip joint   n.) low-class nightclub or restaurant that overcharges people (85)

clockwatcher   n.) person in a hurry to leave work (12)

close shave   n.) narrow escape (95)

clotheshorse   n.) a conspicuously well-dressed person (3)

coast is clear., The   No enemy is in sight. (32)

cock and bull story   n.) an exaggerated or false story (21)

come a long way   v.) make great progress (26)

come across   v.) find or meet by chance (44)

come apart at the seams   v.) be upset and lose control (36)

come clean   v.) tell the truth (38)

come hell or high water   adv.) no matter what happens (77)

Come off it.   Stop kidding, boasting or making believe. (68)

come through (pass) with flying colors   v.) succeed, win, exceed (25)

comeback   n.) an attempt to reclaim a respected position, be successful again (90)

con   v.) lie, swindle, trick (92)

cook someone's goose   v.) create big problems for someone (100)

cough up   v.) give money unwillingly; give up a secret (53)

count on   v.) depend, rely on; trust (12)

cover for someone   v.) protect someone (83)

crack down   v.) become more strict (42)

cream of the crop   n.) the best of a group, top choice (18)

creeps, the   n.) revulsion, fear, uneasiness (88)

crop up   v.) happen quickly without warning (12)

cross one's mind   v.) think of, occur quickly to someone (73)

cue someone in   v.) explain (99)

cut corners   v.) limit one's buying (3)

cut down on   v.) use less, reduce (3)

cut out   adj.) suited to, have talent for (20)

cut out   v.) leave (25)

cut someone down to size   v.) prove someone is not as good as he or she thinks (81)

dawn on   v.) become clear, begin to understand (82)

dead-end job   n.) position with no future (36)

dig up   v.) find, recall, discover (56)

dime a dozen, a   n.) common, easily obtained (33)

dish out   v.) criticize, abuse, scold (61)

dive   n.) a disreputable, low-class bar or nightclub (31)

do something rash   v.) take drastic action (65)

do the trick   v.) be successful, achieve a good result (70)

do without   v.) live without something (5)

doctor up   v.) fix superficially or temporarily (55)

double-check   v.) reinvestigate thoroughly, look again for errors (27)

double-cross   v.) betray (75)

dough   n.) money (53)

down and out   adj.) having no money, no success (9)

down in the dumps   adj.) unhappy (92)

down the drain (tubes)   adj. or adv.) wasted, lost (2)

down-to-earth   adj.) having good sense, practical, unpretentious (45)

draw the line   v.) set a limit (59)

dress up   v.) wear one's best clothes (3)

dribs and drabs   n.) small quantities, little by little (23)

drive at   v.) try to say, insinuate (83)

drive someone up a wall   v.) make someone crazy (60)

drop in the bucket, a   n.) a small amount (10)

drop out, a   n.) one who doesn't complete a study course (25)

drown one's sorrows   v.) drink liquor to forget unhappiness (31)

dump   v.) get rid of, reject (50)

dwell on   v.) talk and think about something all the time (69)

eager beaver   n.) ambitious, zealous, hard worker (12)

earful   n.) especially interesting gossip, information (73)

egg someone on   v.) urge, excite, push (69)

elbow grease   n.) strength for cleaning (57)

elbow room   n.) enough space to be comfortable (56)

end up   v.) finish (27)

every Tom, Dick and Harry   n.) the average person, nobody special (72)

face the music   v.) meet one's punishment, accept the consequences (100)

face up to   v.) accept something unpleasant or difficult (8)

fair and square   adj. or adv.) honest; honestly (64)

fall apart   v.) deteriorate; stop working properly (53)

fall behind   v.) not be able to keep up, fail to maintain a schedule or rate of speed (8)

fall for   v.) begin to love, have strong emotions for (49)

fall for   v.) believe a false story (92)

fall off (drop off)   v.) decrease (33)

fall through   v.) fail, collapse (29)

false alarm   n.) warning or report that's untrue (48)

far-fetched   adj.) exaggerated, unlikely (77)

fast buck   n.) money obtained easily and often unethically (21)

feather in one's cap   n.) proud achievement (14)

feather one's nest   v.) obtain extra money, often dishonestly, through one's job or position (21)

fed up with   adj.) disgusted with, had enough of (2)

feel in one's bones   v.) feel certain without evidence, know by intuition (83)

feel like two cents   v.) feel ashamed or embarrassed (100)

feel sorry for   v.) pity (5)

fender-bender   n.) dent in the fender; minor accident (68)

fiddle around   v.) work without a definite plan or knowledge (55)

figure out   v.) try to understand, solve (71)

fill someone in   v.) tell a person the details (73)

find fault   v.) complain, criticize (72)

fishy   adj.) suspicious, false-sounding (97)

fix one's wagon   v.) make trouble for someone, retaliate (52)

fix someone up   v.) arrange a date for (50)

flip one's lid   v.) get angry; go crazy; become very excited (62)

floor someone   v.) surprise, confuse (73)

flop/turkey   n.) failure (86)

fly off the handle   v.) get angry (8)

fly the coop   v.) leave suddenly, run away (91)

fly-by-night   adj.) unreliable, untrustworthy (27)

foot in the door   n.) opening; hopeful beginning of success (34)

foot the bill   v.) pay (2)

for a song   adv.) at a low price, cheap (89)

for the birds   adj.) terrible, awful (28)

for the time being adv.) at the present time (6)

free-for-all n.) mayhem, disorder (94)

freeload v.) get things that others pay for (1)

from hunger adj.) terrible, bad (90)

from left field adv.) unexpectedly; with an odd or unclear connection to the subject (40)

from scratch adv.) from the very beginning; starting with raw materials (56)

fume v.) be angry (69)

fur will fly, make the fur fly, the v.) create a disturbance (63)

gall n.) shameless, insolent attitude (67)

game adj.) willing, ready (23)

get a grip on oneself v.) take control of one's feelings (37)

get a kick out of v.) enjoy (43)

get a load of v.) have a good look at (43)

get ahead v.) become successful (12)

get along v.) manage (5)

get around to v.) finally find time to do something (15)

get at v.) mean, hint (61)

get away with murder v.) not be punished for wrongdoing (82)

get cold feet v.) be afraid at the last minute, lose confidence (36)

get down to brass tacks v.) begin important work or business (23)

get even v.) get revenge, settle the score (62)

get (give) the runaround v.) be sent from place to place without getting the information needed (80)

get in on the ground floor v.) start from the beginning so you'll have full advantage of any favorable outcome (24)

get in the swing of things v.) adapt or adjust to a new environment (20)

get off one's back v.) leave someone alone, don't bother (59)

get off (start off) on the wrong foot v.) make a bad start (81)

get off the ground v.) make progress, a good start (17)

get one down v.) depress (36)

get one's goat v.) make someone disgusted, annoyed, angry (61)

get out from under v.) end a worrisome situation (9)

get out of v.) withdraw (27)

get out of hand v.) lose control (93)

get something off one's chest v.) unburden oneself; tell what's bothering you (74)

get the ax v.) be fired (99)

get the brush-off v.) be ignored or dismissed (34)

get the show on the road v.) start a project or work (72)

get to first base v.) make a good start, succeed, make progress (25)

get to the bottom of v.) find out the real cause (66)

get under someone's skin v.) annoy, bother, upset (38)

get up and go n.) ambition, energy, enthusiasm (50)

get up on the wrong side of the bed v.) be in a bad mood (41)

get what is coming to one v.) get what one deserves—good or bad (66)

get wind of v.) find out, hear gossip or rumors about (24)

gin mill, a n.) a cheap bar or nightclub (87)

give a hoot (neg.) v.) care (65)

give (get) the cold shoulder v.) be unfriendly to, ignore (45)

give in v.) do as others want, surrender (43)

give it one's best shot v.) try very hard (42)

give someone a break v.) give someone an opportunity or chance (20)

give someone a dose of his or her own medicine v.) treat someone the same way he or she treats others (66)

give someone a hand v.) help (72)

give someone a piece of one's mind v.) say what you really think when angry (47)

give someone his or her walking papers v.) dismiss, fire; send away (78)

give someone the slip v.) escape, get away from (32)

go cold turkey v.) stop abruptly (58)

go down swinging v.) lose but fight until the end (67)

go Dutch v.) each pay for himself or herself (1)

go from bad to worse v.) deteriorate (76)

go out of one's way v.) make a special effort, do more than necessary (72)

go over v.) examine (8)

go over big v.) be very successful (40)

go overboard v.) overact, be reckless (39)

go steady v.) go out with only one person romantically (49)

go to bat for v.) assist, help (75)

go to pieces v.) become crazy, hysterical; lose control of oneself (76)

go to pot v.) deteriorate; become undisciplined, unkempt (56)

go under the knife v.) have surgery (76)

go up in smoke v.) disappear, fail to materialize (40)

go-getter n.) ambitious person (26)

gold mine, a n.) worth a lot of money, successful (89)

goner n.) someone in a lot of trouble (40)

good sport n.) person who loses well (4)

goof off v.) not want to work, be lazy (12)

grab 40 winks v.) take a nap (28)

grand n.) $1,000 (6)

grease monkey n.) automobile mechanic (93)

greasy spoon n.) inexpensive restaurant with mediocre food (85)

great adj.) terrific, wonderful (3)

gung ho adj.) enthusiastic, eager (15)

guts n.) courage (75)

guy n.) man (12)

half-baked adj.) foolish, silly (11)

hand it to someone v.) acknowledge, give credit to (16)

hand over fist adv.) rapidly (21)

hand to mouth adv. or adj.) barely able to cover daily expenses (9)

handful, a n.) a lot of trouble (43)

handle with kid gloves v.) be very careful, tactful (34)

handout n.) charity (9)

handy adj.) can fix things; useful (53)

hang in there v.) be patient, wait (13)

hard feelings n.) anger, bitterness (69)

hard (tough) nut to crack n.) something difficult to do or understand (39)

hard up adj.) in desperate need of something (10)

harp on v.) dwell on one subject, repeat, persist (60)

has-been n.) person once popular but no longer in public favor (90)

hassle v.) bother (79)

have a ball v.) enjoy one's self, have a good time (1)

have a crush on v.) be attracted to (50)

have a fit v.) become upset (53)

have a go at v.) to try, often after others have failed (90)

have a head on one's shoulders v.) be smart or sensible (26)

have a mind of one's own v.) be able to think independently (47)

have a prayer (neg.) v.) have a chance (35)

have another guess (think) coming v.) be mistaken (100)

have been around v.) to be experienced, sophisticated (74)

have egg on one's face v.) be embarrassed (11)

have it coming v.) deserve a punishment (98)

have it made v.) be sure of success, have everything (4)

have it out with someone v.) discuss a conflict or misunderstanding with the other person involved (62)

have one's feet on the ground v.) be practical, sensible, stable (18)

have one's hand in the till v.) steal from one's employer (99)

have one's head in the clouds v.) be daydreaming, lost in thought (16)

have one's heart set on v.) desire greatly (29)

have someone's number v.) know what kind of person someone is (81)

have something up one's sleeve v.) keep secretly ready for the right time (23)

have sticky fingers v.) be a thief (94)

have the heart to (neg.) v.) be pitiless or thoughtless enough (38)

have two strikes against one v.) be in a difficult situation with little chance of success (26)

haywire adj.) broken, confused, awry (55)

heart-to-heart adj.) intimate, honest (74)

hemmed in adj.) crowded, cramped, uncomfortable (56)

high and dry adv. or adj.) alone without help, stranded (96)

high and low adv.) every place (54)

high-brow n.) intellectual, cultured person (31)

hit n.) a success (86)

hit below the belt v.) hurt someone cruelly and unfairly (67)

hit it off v.) enjoy one another's company, get along (45)

hit the bottle v.) drink alcohol (58)

hit the ceiling v.) get angry (4)

hit the nail on the head v.) arrive at the correct answer, make a precise analysis (43)

hit the sack v.) go to bed (54)

hit the skids v.) come upon bad times (31)

hit the spot v.) refresh or satisfy (87)

hogwash n.) nonsense (83)

hold a grudge v.) not forgive someone for an insult or injury (29)

hold back v.) conceal, hide (74)

hold one's horses v.) wait (77)

hold up v.) delay, postpone (70)

hook, line and sinker adv.) without question or doubt (80)

horse sense n.) practical intelligence (95)

hot adj.) stolen (also means "in great demand": he's the **hottest** actor in town) (92)

hot air n.) nonsense or exaggerated talk (80)

hound v.) continually bother, go after (59)

hush-hush adj.) secret (79)

hustler n.) person who gets money aggressively or unethically (21)

hyper adj.) very energetic, anxious, unable to sit still (37)

ill at ease adj.) uncomfortable (91)

in a bind adv.) in trouble no matter what you do (96)

in a huddle adj.) conferring confidentially (76)

in a jam adj.) in trouble (27)

in a nutshell adv.) briefly (91)

in a pinch adv.) okay when nothing else is available (6)

in a rush adj. or adv.) in a hurry (70)

in a rut adj.) always doing the same thing (44)

in advance adv.) ahead of time (86)

in black and white adj.) in writing (41)

in Dutch adj.) in trouble (79)

in hot water adj.) in trouble (43)

in nothing flat adv.) quickly, in a short time (68)

in seventh heaven adv.) very happy (16)

in someone's shoes adv.) in another person's place or position (15)

in stitches adj.) laughing (43)

in the bag adj.) certain, sure, definite (18)

in the chips adj.) having plenty of money (5)

in the doghouse adj.) in trouble (70)

in the klink adj.) in jail (32)

in the long run adv.) in the end, as a result (13)

in the market for adj.) wanting or ready to buy (6)

in the red adv. or adj.) losing money (27)

in the same boat adv. or adj.) in a similar situation (59)

in there pitching adj.) making an effort, trying (22)

iron out v.) work out (34)

jack up v.) raise prices (94)

jack-of-all-trades n.) person who can do many kinds of work (31)

jalopy n.) old car usually in poor condition (6)

jam-packed adj.) crowded, full (86)

jitters, the n.) anxiety, nervousness (88)

John Hancock n.) signature (27)

jump down someone's throat v.) criticize angrily, hastily (64)

jump (get) (climb) on the bandwagon v.) join a popular activity (24)

jump the gun v.) start before you should (17)

jump to conclusions v.) make quick but unjustified conclusions (71)

keep a stiff upper lip v.) have courage, be brave (76)

keep in touch v.) communicate, talk or write to each other (44)

keep on v.) continue (58)

keep one's fingers crossed v.) wish for good luck (16)

keep one's head above water v.) be able to exist on one's income, pay bills (10)

keep one's nose clean v.) stay out of trouble (100)

keep one's nose to the grindstone v.) always work hard, keep busy (18)

keep one's shirt on v.) be patient, wait (72)

keep something under one's hat v.) keep something secret (99)

keep tabs on v.) watch, check (52)

keep up with the Joneses v.) try to equal your neighbors' lifestyle (7)

keyed up adj.) tense, anxious, nervous (37)

kick in the pants (teeth) n.) rejection, criticism (64)

kick oneself v.) regret, be sorry for (78)

kick something around v.) discuss, think about (17)

kick the bucket v.) die (36)

kid n.) young person (43)

kid around v.) fool, play, joke (25)

kiss something goodbye v.) see something ruined or lost (55)

kit and caboodle n.) the entire amount, all (96)

knock it off v.) stop (59)

knock off v.) kill, leave, stop (88)

knock one dead v.) greatly impress, surprise (16)

knock one for a loop v.) surprise (91)

knock one's head against the wall v.) waste time in futile effort to improve or change something (64)

knock oneself out v.) make a great effort (35)

knockout, a n.) a beautiful person or thing (51)

know if one is coming or going (neg.) v.) be able to think clearly, know what to do (37)

know-how n.) experience and knowledge (93)

kosher adj.) true, authentic, right (94)

land on one's feet v.) come out of a bad situation successfully (22)

last straw, the n.) the last insult or injury that one can endure (63)

lay out v.) spend or pay (87)

lead on v.) insincerely encourage (51)

lead one around by the nose v.) have full control of, make someone do what you want (47)

learn the ropes v.) acquire special knowledge of a job (20)

leave someone holding the bag v.) put someone in an awkward position, leave someone else to take blame (75)

lemon n.) merchandise that doesn't work (53)

Let bygones be bygones. Forget differences that happened in the past. (62)

let grass grow under one's feet (neg.) v.) waste time, be lazy (22)

let it ride v.) continue without changing a situation (15)

let on v.) reveal, inform, tell (29)

let one's hair down v.) be informal, relaxed (74)

let someone off v.) excuse from a penalty or promise, permit to leave (98)

let the cat out of the bag v.) tell a secret (69)

Let the chips fall where they may. Act regardless of consequences. (82)

like a ton of bricks adv.) strongly, forcefully (49)

live high off the hog v.) have many luxuries, be very comfortable (22)

live it up v.) pursue pleasure, have a good time (44)

live wire n.) active, exciting person (50)

loaded adj.) having lots of money (1)

loaded adj.) drunk (84)

look down one's nose at v.) think someone is worthless or unimportant, show contempt (46)

look into v.) investigate, check (70)

look up v.) improve, get better (20)

looney bin n.) insane asylum (60)

loot n.) money (56)

lose one's marbles v.) go insane, act irrationally (37)

lose one's shirt v.) lose all one's money (4)

lose track of someone v.) lose contact, not know where someone is (44)

louse up v.) ruin (34)

lowdown n.) the true story (73)

lower the boom v.) stop completely; punish strictly (66)

lulu n.) a person with unconventional, exaggerated behavior; an eccentric character (65)

make a bundle v.) make a lot of money (4)

make a dent in v.) make progress (30)

make a federal case out of something v.) overreact, take strong measures for a minor problem (65)

make a go of v.) succeed, produce good results (89)

make a hit v.) be successful (16)

make a killing v.) gain a large amount of money at one time (7)

make a monkey out of someone v.) cause to look foolish (62)

make a mountain out of a molehill v.) make a big problem out of a small one (63)

make ends meet v.) balance one's budget, meet one's payments (3)

make fun of v.) ridicule (63)

make it up to someone v.) compensate for an unfulfilled promise or debt (29)

make of something v.) interpret, figure out, think of (73)

make one's hair stand on end v.) frighten, horrify (39)

make one's own way v.) rely on one's own abilities (19)

make out v.) do, progress, succeed (93)

make sense v.) be comprehensible (71)

make sure v.) see about something yourself, check (34)

make the best of v.) accept a bad situation and do as well as possible under the circumstances (48)

make up one's mind v.) decide (49)

make waves v.) upset the status quo, create a disturbance (63)

man-to-man adj.) frank, direct (62)

mean business v.) be serious (16)

mess n.) disorderly, cluttered condition; bad or confused situation (54)

miss a trick (neg.) v.) take advantage of every situation (95)

miss out on v.) lose an opportunity, miss a worthwhile event (85)

miss the boat v.) lose an opportunity (25)

mobbed adj.) crowded (86)

mooch v.) borrow, beg, get without paying (9)

moola n.) money (10)

mouthful, a n.) a true and impressive statement (68)

mudslinging n.) making malicious remarks to damage someone's reputation (67)

Mum's the word. Don't talk about what was said. (83)

murder n.) a difficult or painful ordeal (28)

nag, a n.) a persistently urging person (59)

name someone after v.) give a child the name of an admired person (46)

nest egg n.) extra money saved (7)

nightcap, a n.) last drink one has before leaving or sleeping (87)

nincompoop n.) a stupid person, a fool (41)

nip in the bud v.) prevent at the start (63)

nitpick v.) look for very minor errors or problems (60)

nitty-gritty n.) the essence or important part (23)

nitwit n.) idiot (11)

no bed of roses n.) uncomfortable, unhappy situation (30)

No dice. No. Certainly not. (96)

no picnic adj.) not pleasant (13)

nobody's fool n.) smart, competent person (46)

Not on your life. Definitely not, no way. (62)

not so hot adj.) not very good (22)

nothing to sneeze at n.) something not trivial, to be taken seriously (97)

nuts about adj.) in love with, enthusiastic about (51)

odds and ends n.) miscellaneous items (2)

off and on adv.) occasionally (46)

off base adj.) inaccurate (41)

off one's rocker adj.) crazy (30)

off the hook adj. or adv.) out of trouble, freed from an embarrassing situation (77)

off the record adv.) privately, unofficially, not for public announcement (15)

off the top of one's head adv.) from memory, spontaneously (35)

old flame n.) former girlfriend or boyfriend (49)

on a shoestring adv.) with very little money (14)

on easy street adv.) having a pleasant, secure life (89)

on guard adj.) careful, wary (94)

on one's last legs adj.) at the end of one's strength or usefulness (55)

on one's shoulders adj. or adv.) one's responsibility (7)

on pins and needles adj.) nervous, excited (7)

on shaky ground adj.) unstable (48)

on the ball adj.) paying attention and doing things well (18)

on the blink adj.) not working (53)

on the edge of one's seat adj.) in nervous suspense (88)

on the fritz adj.) not working correctly, out of order (55)

on the go adj.) busy running around (28)

on the gravy train adj.) making a lot of money (23)

on the house adj.) provided free by a bar or restaurant (89)

on the level adj.) honest (27)

on the q.t. adv.) secretly (79)

on the rocks adj.) breaking up, ruined (48)

on the same wavelength adj.) communicating, thinking similarly (48)

on the spot adj. or adv.) in a difficult or embarrassing situation (38)

on the wagon adj.) abstaining from liquor (84)

on the warpath adj.) very angry, looking for trouble (65)

once in a blue moon adv.) occasionally; rarely (72)

once-over n.) a quick look or examination (93)

one for the books n.) very unusual, remarkable (11)

one's cup of tea (neg.) n.) something one enjoys, special interest (91)

One's hands are tied. One is unable to help. (19)

One's heart is in one's mouth. One is nervous, fearful, or anxious. (32)

one-track mind n.) mind focused on a single idea (59)

out of line adj.) not usual, incorrect, unacceptable (52)

out of sorts adj.) in a bad mood, irritable (41)

out of the blue adv.) unexpectedly, by surprise, from nowhere (14)

out of the woods adj.) no longer in danger, in the clear (76)

out of this world adj.) wonderful, terrific (23)

out on a limb adj. or adv.) in a dangerous, exposed position; one's ideas are openly known (32)

over a barrel adv.) in a helpless, trapped position (98)

over one's dead body adv.) under no condition, never (93)

pad n.) apartment (57)

pad the bill v.) add false expenses (85)

pain in the neck n.) bothersome, annoying thing or person (70)

palm off v.) sell or get rid of by trickery (96)

pan out v.) happen favorably (16)

pass away v.) die (76)

pass out v.) faint (85)

pass the buck v.) shift responsibility to others (41)

pat on the back, a n.) praise (25)

patch up v.) fix (58)

pay through the nose v.) pay too much (28)

peanuts n.) a small amount of money (96)

pep talk n.) a talk to arouse enthusiasm (15)

perk up v.) emerge from a depressed or uninterested mood (87)

pick up v.) obtain, get (2)

pick up the tab v.) pay the bill (1)

pick-me-up, a n.) a drink or snack taken to refresh oneself (87)

piece of cake, a n.) easy (11)

pile up v.) accumulate; put things on top of each other (54)

pill n.) an annoying, disagreeable person (60)

pin someone down v.) make someone tell the truth or agree to something (41)

pinch pennies v.) be thrifty, careful how you spend money (9)

pink slip n.) notice of dismissal (15)

pinpoint v.) find exact location or cause (39)

pitch in v.) help (12)

pits, the n.) the worst, anything that is very bad (81)

play hooky v.) stay away from school or work without permission (13)

play it by ear v.) make your decision according to the situation (34)

play the field v.) go out with many people romantically (49)

play up to someone v.) flatter or please for selfish reasons (51)

play with fire v.) invite danger, trouble (51)

plenty of adj.) a lot of, abundant (84)

point out v.) explain, show, call attention to (93)

pop the question v.) ask to marry (49)

pound the pavement v.) look for a job (38)

pour (spread, put, lay) it on thick v.) flatter profusely, exaggerate (51)

pretty penny n.) a lot of money (24)

pull a fast one v.) cheat, deceive (93)

pull a number on v.) cheat, deceive (97)

pull punches v.) hide unpleasant facts or make them seem good (80)

pull someone's leg v.) trick, playfully tease, fool (20)

pull something off v.) accomplish something remarkable (35)

pull strings v.) secretly use influence and power (19)

pull the rug out from under v.) spoil someone's plans, withdraw support (99)

pull the wool over one's eyes v.) deceive, mislead (95)

pull up stakes v.) move to another location (39)

push someone around v.) boss, make a person do what you want (52)

put a damper on v.) discourage, spoil a person's fun (50)

put anything past someone (neg.) v.) be surprised by what someone does (78)

put down v.) make someone look bad, criticize (47)

put in one's two cents v.) give one's opinion (19)

put one out v.) inconvenience, bother (72)

put one's cards on the table v.) be frank, tell everything (75)

put one's finger on v.) find precisely, remember exactly (39)

put one's foot down v.) object strongly, take firm preventive action (47)

put one's foot in one's mouth v.) speak carelessly, make a rude or insensitive comment (34)

put our heads together v.) confer, discuss (79)

put someone in his or her place v.) scold someone for rude, improper behavior (65)

put someone on v.) tease, pretend, exaggerate (45)

put someone on a pedestal v.) idolize, worship (51)

put something out of one's head (mind) v.) try not to think about (79)

put something over on someone v.) fool (99)

put the bite on someone v.) ask for a loan of money (21)

put through the wringer v.) cause severe stress (67)

put two and two together v.) make a conclusion knowing the facts (95)

put up a good front v.) pretend to be happy, fool people about one's status (10)

put up with v.) patiently accept, endure (52)

quack n.) an ignorant or fraudulent doctor (80)

rack one's brains v.) try hard to think or remember (10)
racket n.) easy, well-paying job; business that cheats customers (93)
raise Cain v.) create a disturbance, make trouble (29)
raise eyebrows v.) cause surprise or disapproval, shock (91)
rake it in v.) make a lot of money (4)
rake over the coals v.) scold, reprimand, blame (67)
rat race n.) endless, competitive striving; hurried, material existence (36)
raw deal n.) unfair treatment (98)
read between the lines v.) understand things that are not said, find a hidden meaning (71)
real McCoy n.) the genuine thing (96)
right off the bat adv.) in the beginning, immediately (95)
right under one's nose adv.) in an obvious, nearby place (54)
ring a bell v.) remind one of something familiar (97)
rip off v.) cheat, rob (92)
road hog n.) person who takes too much room on the road (68)
rock the boat v.) upset the status quo (82)
rope into v.) trick, persuade, or pressure (28)
rough adj.) approximate (41)
rub one the wrong way v.) annoy, bother, make angry (18)
rub something in v.) constantly refer to a mistake or fault (64)
rule out v.) decide against, eliminate (88)
rule the roost v.) be the dominant one in the family (52)
run around in circles v.) act confused, do a lot but accomplish little (37)
run out of v.) finish the supply, use up (2)
run ragged v.) tire, exhaust (28)
run (take) a risk v.) be open to danger or loss, unprotected (80)
run-down adj.) in bad condition (57)

sail into v.) get angry verbally (78)
salt away v.) save, keep hidden until needed (7)
say (cry) "uncle" v.) admit defeat (67)
scalper n.) a person who buys a ticket

at the regular rate and sells it at a profit (86)
scam n.) a plan to cheat someone (97)
scatter around v.) carelessly put in different places (54)
scrape the bottom of the barrel v.) take whatever is left after best has been taken (81)
scrape together v.) get money little by little (53)
scratch the surface v.) merely begin to understand or accomplish something (73)
scrounge around v.) look in a lot of places for a certain item (56)
second-hand adj.) not new, previously used (56)
see daylight v.) achieve or expect a favorable result (10)
see eye to eye v.) have the same opinion, agree (47)
see through v.) understand the true character of someone or something (95)
sell like hotcakes v.) sell quickly, rapidly (94)
sell oneself short v.) underestimate oneself (36)
send someone packing v.) tell someone to leave, dismiss (99)
serve someone right v.) give due punishment (64)
serve time (do time) v.) be in jail (94)
set one back v.) cost (6)
set someone up v.) put someone in a position to be manipulated (97)
settle down v.) live a quiet, normal life (44)
settle the score v.) retaliate, pay someone back for a past hurt (62)
shape up v.) begin to act and look right (15)
sharp adj.) smart, witty, quick-thinking (21)
shell out v.) pay (87)
shook up adj.) upset, worried, fearful (88)
shoot full of holes v.) find great fault with (42)
shoot the breeze v.) talk idly or gossip (38)
shop around v.) look in many stores (3)
shoplifter n.) one who steals goods from stores (94)
short end of the stick n.) unfair, unequal treatment (64)
shrug off v.) not be bothered or hurt, dismiss (63)
sick and tired adj.) disliking some continual behavior, annoyed (80)
side with v.) favor, support one position in a dispute (75)

side-swipe v.) hit the side of a car (68)
simmer down v.) become calm, quiet (37)
sink one's teeth into v.) go to work seriously (23)
sink or swim v.) fail or succeed by your own efforts (90)
sit right (neg.) v.) be acceptable (60)
sit tight v.) wait patiently (9)
sitting pretty adj.) in a favorable situation (13)
6 feet under adj.) dead (86)
size of it, the n.) the way it is (45)
size up v.) form an opinion, assess (92)
skeleton in one's closet n.) a family secret (83)
skip v.) forget, pass over (2)
sky-high adj.) expensive (3)
sleazy adj.) shoddy, dirty, in poor condition (31)
sleep on it v.) think about, consider, decide later (82)
sling hash v.) be a waitress (22)
slip one's mind v.) be forgotten (77)
slob n.) person who isn't clean and neat (54)
smack into v.) collide, hit (68)
smell a rat v.) become suspicious (96)
smooth something over v.) make better or more pleasant (42)
snap, a n.) an easy task (35)
snap out of it v.) free oneself from the control of panic, fear, hysteria, etc. (76)
snow job n.) insincere or exaggerated talk intended to trick or impress (92)
snowball's chance in hell, a n.) no chance at all (21)
sob story n.) sad story that makes the listener sympathetic (97)
soft touch n.) one who gives money easily when asked (21)
song and dance n.) excuses (42)
sore loser n.) person who gets angry when he loses (4)
sort of adv.) almost, not quite; like, similar to; rather (25)
sourpuss n.) a disagreeable person who seldom smiles (52)
spic and span adj.) very clean, very neat (57)
spill the beans v.) tell a secret, inform (13)
spine-chilling adj.) terrifying, thrilling (88)
spitting image n.) exact resemblance (46)
split hairs v.) make trivial, unnecessary distinctions (60)
split up v.) separate (48)
splurge v.) spend a lot of money for something (1)

spoiled adj.) getting and expecting everything one wants (43)

sport n.) person generous with money (89)

spring v.) pay (89)

spruce up v.) clean, redecorate (56)

square one n.) the beginning (40)

squawk about v.) complain about (7)

squeal v.) inform (38)

stab someone in the back v.) betray someone (78)

stand (neg.) v.) tolerate, like (18)

stand on one's own two feet v.) be independent (42)

stand someone up v.) fail to keep an appointment or date (50)

stand up to someone v.) be brave, courageously confront someone (66)

start the ball rolling v.) take the initiative, begin an action (66)

stay away from v.) avoid (84)

steer clear of someone v.) avoid (46)

stick one's neck out v.) look for trouble, take risks (32)

stick it out v.) endure, continue (91)

stick to one's guns v.) to defend an action or opinion despite an unfavorable reaction (16)

stick up for v.) defend, help, support (47)

stink v.) to be of extremely bad quality, to be terrible (33)

straight from the horse's mouth adv.) directly from the person involved (24)

straight from the shoulder adv.) open and honest way of speaking (80)

straighten out (up) v.) put in order (54)

strapped adj.) having no money available (22)

strike while the iron is hot v.) take advantage of an opportunity (14)

strings attached n.) restraining circumstances, obligations (95)

stuck adj.) unable to understand, remember, or solve; unable to move (71)

stuff n.) things (56)

stuffed shirt n.) a person who is rigid or too formal (81)

swamped adj.) overwhelmed (13)

swan song n.) final appearance (90)

sweat bullets v.) be nervous; be very hot (35)

sweatshop n.) a factory that has poor conditions, long hours, low pay (22)

swell adj.) terrific (45)

take a beating v.) lose money (14)

take a crack at v.) try, attempt (22)

take a powder v.) leave quickly, run away (59)

take advantage of v.) treat unfairly for your own gain; make good use of time or conditions (71)

take after v.) resemble or act like a parent or relative (46)

take it v.) endure trouble, criticism, abuse, pressure (61)

take on v.) begin to handle, commit oneself to, accept (20)

take one's hat off to someone v.) admire, respect, praise (26)

take over (take charge) v.) take control, command (17)

take someone for a ride v.) cheat, swindle (28)

take someone to the cleaners v.) win all of someone's money, cheat someone (4)

take something lying down v.) suffer without a fight (67)

take something to heart v.) consider seriously (60)

take the bull by the horns v.) take strong action (25)

take the Fifth v.) refuse to testify against oneself, as guaranteed by the Fifth Amendment to the Constitution (98)

take the plunge v.) do something decisive (17)

take the words out of someone's mouth v.) say something someone else was going to say (75)

take up v.) begin an activity or hobby (70)

take with a grain of salt v.) listen with skepticism (11)

talk through one's hat v.) make exaggerated or inaccurate statements (11)

talk turkey v.) discuss seriously, in a business-like manner (36)

tearjerker n.) story that makes you cry (86)

teetotaler n.) person who never drinks liquor (84)

tell someone off v.) speak to angrily (78)

That ain't hay! That's a lot of money. (6)

think up v.) invent, create (17)

third degree, the n.) prolonged questioning (38)

through the grapevine adv.) via gossip from other people (78)

through the mill adj.) experienced in difficulties of life (14)

throw cold water on v.) discourage (42)

throw in the towel v.) surrender, give up (33)

throw one's weight around v.) use one's influence in a showy manner (19)

throw the book at v.) punish severely for breaking rules or the law (98)

tickled pink adj.) very happy (77)

tide someone over v.) help someone through a shortage (8)

tie the knot v.) get married (84)

tied down adj.) restricted by family or job responsibilities (44)

tight squeeze n.) difficult situation financially (96)

tighten one's belt v.) economize, spend and use less (5)

tightwad n.) person who is cheap and stingy (77)

tip someone off v.) warn, inform (78)

to a T adv.) perfectly, exactly (19)

to boot adv.) in addition, also (26)

to the hilt adv.) completely, to the limit (8)

tooth and nail adv.) as hard as possible, fiercely (98)

top-notch adj.) excellent, the best (31)

topsy-turvy adj.) upside down, in disarray (57)

total v.) completely ruin (68)

touch and go adj.) very dangerous or uncertain (80)

tough break n.) unlucky event, misfortune (31)

tourist trap n.) any place that is overpriced and attracts tourists (85)

track down v.) search for (44)

treat v.) pay for someone else (1)

try something out v.) test (17)

turn one off v.) disgust, bore, repel (45)

turn out v.) result, end (29)

turn over a new leaf v.) change one's conduct for the better (58)

turn someone down v.) reject (49)

turn someone's stomach v.) get someone sick and upset (57)

turn the tables v.) reverse the situation (66)

turn to v.) go to for help (9)

turn up v.) appear (54)

twiddle one's thumbs v.) not busy, not working (33)

twist someone around one's finger v.) influence someone easily (51)

two-faced adj.) disloyal, untrustworthy (78)

under the table adv.) illegal money transaction, such as paying a bribe (57)

under the weather adj.) not feeling well (13)

up one's alley adj.) something one enjoys, special interest (91)

米語イディオム練習帳
IDIOMATIC AMERICAN ENGLISH

1986年 3 月15日　　第 1 刷発行
1998年 4 月15日　　第 13 刷発行

著　者　　バーバラ・ゲインズ

発行者　　野間佐和子

発行所　　講談社インターナショナル株式会社
　　　　　〒112-8652 東京都文京区音羽 1-17-14
　　　　　電話：03-3944-6493

印刷所　　株式会社　平河工業社

製本所　　株式会社　国宝社

up the river adv.) in jail (98)
up to here with adj.) disgusted with another's continual behavior (38)
up to one's ears adj.) deeply immersed in (30)
up to par (neg.) adv. or adj.) meeting normal standards (42)
up to someone n.) someone's choice (70)
upset the applecart v.) ruin or spoil a plan or idea (79)
use one's noodle (head) v.) think (71)

walk all over someone v.) take advantage of someone (64)
wash one's hands of v.) refuse responsibility for, abandon (32)
washed up adj.) no longer successful or needed; failed (90)
waste one's breath v.) speak or argue with no result (19)
watch (mind) one's P's and Q's v.) act very carefully, pay attention to details (30)
water down v.) dilute (99)

wear the pants v.) be the boss of a family (52)
weigh one's words v.) be careful of what one says (52)
well-heeled adj.) rich (14)
well-off adj.) rich, wealthy (46)
wet behind the ears adj.) inexperienced (92)
wet blanket n.) person who discourages others from having fun (50)
wet one's whistle v.) have a drink, especially alcohol (87)
what it takes n.) any ability for a job; courage (90)
when the chips are down adv.) at the worst time, when one faces the biggest obstacles (9)
whistle a different tune v.) change one's attitude, contradict previous ideas (61)
wild goose chase n.) absurd or hopeless search (57)
will power n.) strength of mind (58)
wimp n.) spineless, non-assertive person (75)

wind up v.) end, finish (14)
wing it v.) rely only on one's knowledge; act without preparation (35)
wisecrack n.) sarcastic or nasty remark (62)
wishy-washy adj.) having no definite opinion; unable to decide (75)
with a fine-tooth comb adv.) very carefully (35)
within reason adv. or adj.) sensible, reasonable; reasonably (39)
word of mouth n.) recommendation from other people (85)
work one's fingers to the bone v.) work very hard (20)
work out v.) find an answer, solve (48)
wrong side of the tracks, the n.) the poor section of town, implying social inferiority (26)

yell (scream) bloody murder v.) express loud, emotional anger (50)
You're kidding! Really? Is it true? (92)

POWER JAPANESE

The Power Japanese series presents a selection of focused, inexpensive guides to difficult or confusing aspects of the Japanese language. Each text in the series is self-contained, addressing a problem or area too large for a single chapter in a textbook, too small for a whole course—and often left out of regular course texts altogether. The student can find a quick reference to particles, a guide to the myriad levels of politeness, books of idioms, vocabulary builders, emotive expressions and turns of speech—all complete and provided with natural and plentiful examples. With levels ranging from the beginning to the advanced, individual problems can be targeted with minimum hassle and expense.

ALL ABOUT KATAKANA
カタカナ練習ノート
Anne Matsumoto Stewart
Learn to read and write katakana in a quick, effective way by combining them into words.
Paperback, 144 pages; ISBN 4-7700-1696-4

ALL ABOUT PARTICLES
助詞で変わるあなたの日本語
Naoko Chino
The most common and less common particles brought together and broken down into some 200 usages, with abundant sample sentences.
Paperback, 128 pages; ISBN 0-87011-954-0

ANIMAL IDIOMS
動物の慣用句集
Jeff Garrison and Masahiko Goshi
A memorable explanation of idioms—all dealing with animals. Organized by zoological category with background notes and sample sentences.
Paperback, 160 pages; ISBN 4-7700-1668-9

BASIC CONNECTIONS
日本語の基礎ルール
Making Your Japanese Flow
Kakuko Shoji
The connective expressions that facilitate the flow of ideas—how words and phrases dovetail, how clauses pair up with other clauses, and how sentences come together to create harmonious paragraphs.
Paperback, 154 pages; ISBN 4-7700-1968-8

BEYOND POLITE JAPANESE
役にたつ話ことば辞典
A Dictionary of Japanese Slang and Colloquialisms
Akihiko Yonekawa
Expressions that all Japanese, but few foreigners, know and use every day. Sample sentences for every entry.
Paperback, 176 pages; ISBN 4-7700-1539-9

"BODY" LANGUAGE
日本語の中の〝ボディ〟ランゲージ
Jeffrey G. Garrison
Common idioms that refer to the body through colorful colloquial expressions.
Paperback, 128 pages; ISBN 0-87011-955-9

COMMON JAPANESE PHRASES
決まり文句の辞典
Compiled by Sanseido
Translated and Adapted by **John Brennan**
The appropriate words—fixed expressions and phrases for every social situation explained in short essay format, complete with tips on culture and alternatives.
Paperback, 144 pages; ISBN 4-7700-2072-4

COMMUNICATING WITH KI
The "Spirit" in Japanese Idioms
「気」の慣用句集
Jeff Garrison and Kayoko Kimiya
Over 200 idioms, all using the word ki, and all essential for communicating in Japanese.
Paperback, 144 pages; ISBN 4-7700-1833-9

FLIP, SLITHER, & BANG
Japanese Sound and Action Words
日本語の擬音語・擬態語
Hiroko Fukuda
Translated and edited by Tom Gally
The most common examples of onomatopoeia through sample sentences and situations—an excellent introduction to animated language.
Paperback, 128 pages; ISBN 4-7700-1684-0

HOW TO SOUND INTELLIGENT IN JAPANESE
日本語の知的表現
Charles M. De Wolf
Lists, defines and gives examples for the vocabulary necessary to engage in intelligent conversations in fields such as, politics, art, literature, business, and science.
Paperback, 144 pages; ISBN 4-7700-1747-2

INSTANT VOCABULARY THROUGH PREFIXES AND SUFFIXES
増えて使えるヴォキャブラリー
Timothy J. Vance
Expand vocabulary and improve reading comprehension by modifying your existing lexicon.
Paperback, 128 pages; ISBN 0-87011-953-2

JAPANESE VERBS AT A GLANCE
日本語の動詞
Naoko Chino
Clear and straightforward explanations of Japanese verbs—their functions, forms, roles, and politeness levels.
Paperback, 180 pages; ISBN 4-7700-1985-8

KANJI IDIOMS
四字熟語
George Wallace and Kayoko Kimiya
Frequently used phrases composed of four kanji characters essential for educated conversation.
Paperback, 160 pages; ISBN 4-7700-1943-2

LIVING JAPANESE
A Modern Reader
楽しく読む日本語
Marc Bookman and Kazuko Fujii
A selection of short fiction and non-fiction articles in Japanese with vocabulary lists, idiomatic expressions and quizzes.
Paperback, 132 pages; ISBN 4-7700-2035-X

LOVE, HATE AND EVERYTHING IN BETWEEN
Expressing Emotions in Japanese
日本語の感情表現集
Mamiko Murakami
Translated by Ralph McCarthy
All the vocabulary and phrases necessary to hit just the right nuance and say exactly what you feel.
Paperback, 170 pages; ISBN 4-7700-2089-9

MAKING SENSE OF JAPANESE
What the Textbooks Don't Tell You
日本語の秘訣
Answers to all those nagging questions of basic Japanese, masterfully handled with a light touch and a good deal of humor. Formerly published as *Gone Fishin'*, now with a new chapter on upside-down sentences.
Paperback, 140 pages; ISBN 4-7700-2310-3

READ REAL JAPANESE
日本語で読もう
Janet Ashby
Ten essays by popular Japanese authors. All vocabulary is defined, and grammar explained so the book can be read without a dictionary.
Paperback, 168 pages; ISBN 4-7700-1754-5

STRANGE BUT TRUE
A True-Life Japanese Reader
デキゴトロジーを読む
Tom Gally
Eight real-life stories packed with humor and oddity. An entertaining introduction to reading Japanese.
Paperback, 140 pages; ISBN 4-7700-2057-0

T-SHIRT JAPANESE VERSUS NECKTIE JAPANESE
Two Levels of Politeness
Tシャツの日本語ネクタイの日本語
Hiroko Fukuda
Translated by Charles M. De Wolf
Paired dialogues expressing the same thoughts demonstrate polite and colloquial language, complete with down-to-earth commentary.
Paperback, 152 pages; ISBN 4-7700-1834-7

KODANSHA INTERNATIONAL DICTIONARIES
Easy-to-use dictionaries designed for non-native learners of Japanese.

ふりがな和英辞典
KODANSHA'S FURIGANA
JAPANESE-ENGLISH DICTIONARY
The essential dictionary for all students of Japanese.
  • Furigana readings added to all Kanji   • Comprehensive 16,000-word basic vocabulary
Vinyl binding, 592 pages, ISBN 4-7700-1983-1

ふりがな英和辞典
KODANSHA'S FURIGANA
ENGLISH-JAPANESE DICTIONARY
The essential dictionary for all students of Japanese.
  • Furigana readings added to all Kanji   • Comprehensive 14,000-word basic vocabulary
Vinyl binding, 728 pages, ISBN 4-7700-2055-4

ポケット版　ローマ字和英辞典
KODANSHA'S POCKET ROMANIZED
JAPANESE-ENGLISH DICTIONARY
Easy-to-use and convenient, an ideal pocket reference for beginning and intermediate students, travelers, and business people.
  • 10,000-word vocabulary.   • Numerous example sentences.
Paperback, 480 pages, ISBN 4-7700-1800-2

ローマ字和英辞典
KODANSHA'S ROMANIZED JAPANESE-ENGLISH DICTIONARY
A portable reference written for beginning and intermediate students of Japanese.
  • 16,000-word vocabulary.   • No knowledge of *kanji* necessary.
Vinyl binding, 688 pages, ISBN 4-7700-1603-4

ポケット版　教育漢英熟語辞典
KODANSHA'S POCKET KANJI GUIDE
A handy, pocket-sized character dictionary designed for ease of use.
  • 1,006 *shin-kyoiku kanji*.   • 10,000 common compounds.
  • Stroke order for individual characters.
Paperback, 576 pages, ISBN 4-7700-1801-0

常用漢英熟語辞典
KODANSHA'S COMPACT KANJI GUIDE
A functional character dictionary that is both compact and comprehensive.
  • 1,945 essential *joyo kanji*.   • 20,000 common compounds.
  • Three indexes for finding *kanji*.
Vinyl binding, 928 pages, ISBN 4-7700-1553-4

日本語学習使い分け辞典
EFFECTIVE JAPANESE USAGE GUIDE
A concise, bilingual dictionary which clarifies the usage of frequently confused Japanese words and phrases.
  • Explanations of 708 synonymous terms.   • Numerous example sentences.
Paperback, 768 pages, ISBN 4-7700-1919-X